HUMAN RELATIONS
IN INTERRACIAL HOUSING

Human Relations in Interracial Housing

IS PUBLISHED WITH SUPPORT FROM THE

EDWARD F. WAITE PUBLICATION FUND

OF THE UNIVERSITY OF MINNESOTA PRESS

This fund was established in 1944 by George B. Leonard of Minneapolis to honor the career of Edward F. Waite, retired judge of the district court in Hennepin County, Minnesota. Throughout a long life of service to the community, Judge Waite has always shown, in word and deed, an admirable social consciousness and a keen appreciation of the importance of friendship and understanding among peoples of all races everywhere.

HUMAN RELATIONS
IN INTERRACIAL HOUSING

A STUDY OF THE CONTACT HYPOTHESIS

Daniel M. Wilner
Rosabelle Price Walkley
Stuart W. Cook

UNIVERSITY OF MINNESOTA PRESS, Minneapolis

PRINTED AT THE COLWELL PRESS, INC., MINNEAPOLIS

Library of Congress Catalog Card Number: 55-9373

PUBLISHED IN GREAT BRITAIN, INDIA, AND PAKISTAN BY
GEOFFREY CUMBERLEGE: OXFORD UNIVERSITY PRESS, LONDON, BOMBAY, AND KARACHI

Foreword

PUBLIC Housing officials in the United States, like many other people, have differed in their views on the social desirability or workability of having white and Negro families live in the same buildings. These different points of view are reflected in the policies and procedures of different city housing authorities, and have resulted in different occupancy patterns in public housing projects.

In recent years more and more housing authorities have contemplated a change from some form of racial *segregation* of tenants to *integration,* in which tenants are located within a project regardless of race. Many have actually altered policy in that direction.

These policy decisions are conditioned by a variety of complex factors. Several can be singled out here. The general social trend of recent years has greatly increased the extent of racial interaction in many areas of endeavor. The changing climate of opinion regarding racial interaction has had an influence on policy makers in public housing agencies, as well as on those in related official and private agencies dealing directly with human problems.

But recognition of a trend does not produce, automatically, specifications for the actions necessary to change existing policies. Policy makers in the housing field should take into account the entire cultural setting in which the new policies are to apply. For example, they should be realistically sensitive to the local political climate and to the views of churches and of other respected groups in the community. Furthermore, there must be co-ordination of plans and activities with those of kindred public agencies, many of which are concerned with the same clients. Finally, the details of strategy for carrying out the new policy must be worked out.

At some point in the thinking and planning for a change in racial policy in housing, a final question arises concerning the immediate consequences of the change on the tenants of both races. The policy maker naturally wonders what impact integration will have on relations among the families occupying the projects for which he is responsible. It is from this point of view that he finds scientific studies like the one reported in this book useful.

Perhaps the basic contribution of the book to those concerned with housing problems is the picture it presents of relations that exist between white and Negro housewives in the four housing projects studied. Of special interest is the detailed account of relations between the Negro and white persons who live closest to one another, as neighbors either in the same building or in adjoining buildings. Among other things the authors have analyzed their evidence in such a way as to trace the process through which interracial adjustments take place. They recount, also, the impact of integration on the feelings and activities of white women who were initially quite hostile to the other race.

These and other findings of the study provide some of the answers to pressing questions concerning the way in which integration works out in actual practice. Northern cities which have segregation in public housing—and there are many—can learn from this book much that will be of direct application to their own public housing problems. Border cities like Baltimore, which are already moving in the direction of ending segregation, as well as numerous southern cities where plans for desegregation may be undertaken in the next few years, will also find the book to be of great value, however different they feel their own interracial situation may be.

What this book has to say is of importance to *all* public housing officials (whatever their geographical location) who recognize that their role is to do more than manage buildings and provide maintenance, and who feel that their procedures make social policy as well as carry it out.

Oliver C. Winston
EXECUTIVE DIRECTOR, HOUSING
AUTHORITY OF BALTIMORE CITY

April 1955

Preface

THIS book reports the second of a program of studies of intergroup relations conducted by the staff of the Research Center for Human Relations. The focus of this program is upon the understanding of conditions underlying the possible behavioral and attitudinal outcomes of social contact between persons from different racial, religious, and national groups. Experience shows that such contact may result either in friendly attitude and behavior or in an exaggeration of existing suspicions and antagonisms.

From the point of view of community life these two diametrically different possibilities pose a dilemma in our efforts to ameliorate irrational social friction. From the point of view of social science they are a challenge to our understanding of the dynamics of attitude change and of the process of social interaction. We have approached research on this problem with the hope of contributing on both the community and the scientific fronts.

In the United States, developments of the last few years have had the effect of rapidly increasing the amount of face-to-face contact between persons from mutually suspicious and antagonistic social groups. The manpower shortage of World War II, for example, led many business firms to employ Negroes in industries which had previously been racially segregated. The war also saw the beginning of racial integration in our armed forces; this change is still in process. Since the war a series of judicial and administrative decisions have resulted in greater racial and religious association in employment, recreation, transportation, housing, education, etc. This trend has reached a high point in the epic-making Supreme Court decision declaring unconstitutional the policy of racial segregation in public schools.

Parallel to the increase in intergroup contact across racial and religious lines in this country, there has been a rapid development in *international* social contact. Stimulated by the various exchange-of-persons programs, students, teachers, businessmen, and others are coming to this country in ever larger numbers. The number of foreign students alone in the United States during the academic year of 1954–55 is estimated to be 30,000. For a time it was generally assumed that the outcome of contact between the foreign visitor and Americans was uniformly favorable. As examples to the contrary accumulated, this assumption gave way to the recognition that a more critical evaluation of the effect of the visitor's experience must be made. It is now generally agreed that, as is the case with interracial contact, such international association may lead under some conditions to more friendly attitudes toward Americans while under other conditions it may lead to increased antagonisms. What these conditions are remains to be determined.

One consequence of this increase in interracial and international contact has been a heightened feeling of uncertainty on the part of those in policy-making and administrative positions. From many quarters come questions reflecting a need for information and guidance. Will integration lead to racial tension and perhaps even to violence? Will contact between foreign visitors and Americans lead to lowered esteem for America and democracy? And if these are possibilities, what can be done to avoid them?

Studies of intergroup contact conducted in public housing, schools and colleges, industry, and other foci of social life may, over a period of time, provide helpful if not complete answers to such questions. For the policy maker and administrator, who too often are in the position of making relatively uninformed guesses about these questions, the findings of such studies should come as a welcome aid.

On the theoretical side, as noted above, we are concerned in this study with the general problem of social interaction and attitude change, of which the outcomes of intergroup contact are a special instance. Although the formation and modification of attitudes has the distinction of being one of the most intensively studied problems in social psychology, it is still in a sense unorganized as a research area. The broad problem of attitude change is, of course, too complex to make possible a single, all-inclusive organized attack upon it. Is it possible to identify some limited category of attitude-change studies that might still provide sufficient material to permit the drawing of tentative conclusions about the dynamics of the change process? It seems to us that the question of change of attitudes toward members of racial, religious, or national groups in situations of intergroup contact constitutes just such a limited area. A considerable body of evidence has been gathered on this question. While the numerous studies which have been carried out cover a wide range of contact situations, the general type of influence being brought to bear (face-to-face contact with other individuals) and the general object of attitudes in question (one or more specific ethnic groups) remain constant.

Interracial Housing: A Psychological Evaluation of a Social Experiment, by Morton Deutsch and Mary Evans Collins, told the story of the first field experiment to be conducted by the Research Center for Human Relations in line with this general approach to the study of attitude change. The present book, as we have said, deals with the second field experiment. A third study, dealing with the outcomes of contact between national groups is, at this writing, nearing completion. The reader will see the many ways in which the intepretation in this book has been enriched through the numerous comparisons with the Deutsch and Collins study. It is our hope that this progressive cumulation of understanding will accelerate as our research program continues.

Stuart W. Cook

DIRECTOR, RESEARCH CENTER FOR HUMAN
RELATIONS, NEW YORK UNIVERSITY

May 1955

Authors' Introduction

Two aspects of the study reported in the following pages deserve special comment. The first has to do with the difficulties encountered in the study's early stages; the second, with the cooperation accorded the study staff by several hundred people from many walks of life and located in many different cities.

As originally conceived, the study was to replicate a previous study*
conducted in public housing developments. However, the housing
projects of the present study were to have characteristics more nearly
representative of housing developments throughout the country than
had been the case in the earlier research. The general plan was to compare the interracial attitudes of two groups of white persons, those
living in integrated and those living in segregated public housing projects. The general task was therefore the location of two pairs of public
housing projects a "considerable" distance from the New York area;
the projects in each pair to be as alike one another as possible in several
important characteristics, and to differ only in that one in each pair
was to have an integrated occupancy pattern and the other, a segregated pattern.

While the search for suitable housing projects was fraught with difficulty, it was not without interest, however, and resembled in some
respects the unraveling of a mystery story. Before the study got under
way, the Public Housing Administration in Washington, D.C., had
made available to the study staff, statistics on the size, age, and ethnic
composition of all *federally* supported low-rental public housing projects in the United States. Examination of these statistics had given
reason to believe that while the search would have to be pursued diligently, there was a good likelihood of locating the two matched pairs
of projects. Proceeding on the basis of the available statistics, the

* Morton Deutsch and Mary Evans Collins, *Interracial Housing*, University of Minnesota Press, 1950.

authors systematically began obtaining the additional information
needed to select comparable projects: this was done through letters,
telephone calls, and personal visits to a number of cities. It soon developed that reports from local housing authorities to the Public
Housing Administration regarding the proportion of Negro and white
residents were sometimes incomplete, and that different authorities
meant different things by "integrated" occupancy pattern. In the latter
connection, for example, a project would be listed as integrated when,
as a matter of fact, further investigation revealed that it was either
building-segregated or area-segregated. The discrepancy often reflected
the conflict between the need to show adherence to the public housing
law, on the one hand, and the realities of local policy on the other. The
end product of this investigation of *federally* supported housing projects yielded only one pair of housing projects that were reasonably well
matched.

We then turned our attention to *state* supported projects. A number
of states east of the Mississippi had in the preceding few years begun
to subsidize public housing, usually for moderate-income families.
After an exhaustive search involving the same general procedures followed with the low-rental federal projects, we located two matched
state-supported moderate-rental projects which had the desired characteristics.

As the search for comparable projects went on, a variable suggested
itself that was to become eventually a primary focus of the study. It
turned out that Negro families numbered about 10 per cent of the total
population in each project, even though we had set out originally to
find projects with at least 25 per cent Negro residents. As a consequence of the low proportion of Negro residents, white residents could
be found in each project living varying distances from Negro residents;
this was the case even in the segregated projects which had turned out
to be building-segregated rather than area-segregated. It became possible, as a result, to make "near"-"far" comparisons among white
tenants in each project—a factor which was to provide considerable
refinement of our understanding of the processes leading to attitude
change.

So much for the difficulties of making experimental comparisons
under field conditions. That we overcame these difficulties was due in
large measure to the many individuals and organizations whose help at
various stages made the study possible. Among these were representa-
tives of housing agencies in Washington and elsewhere who made available information not yet in published reports and who gave us leads
for the selection of projects. We owe a major debt to officials of the

four housing authorities whose projects we studied and to various project personnel whose cooperation made field work a good deal easier than it might otherwise have been. In Springfield, Massachusetts, we wish to thank John I. Robinson, Director of the Springfield Housing Authority, Harold Sjostrum, project manager, and Rita Murphy and Evelyn Kelly, tenant selection officer and assistant, respectively; in Hartford, Connecticut, Goodwin Beach, then Chairman of the Housing Authority of the City of Hartford, and Thomas J. O'Neil, Administrative Assistant; in Philadelphia, Walter F. Allesandroni, Executive Director of the Philadelphia Housing Authority, Drayton Bryant, then Assistant to the Executive Director, and Charles Kircher, project manager; in Pittsburgh, the late Clarence C. Klein, then Administrator of the Housing Authority of Pittsburgh, J. Warren Matson, Applications Office Supervisor, and Robert S. Haas, project manager.

We are indebted, also, to the interviewers who knocked at doors and collected the data which are described in this book. These are too often the unsung heroes (or heroines) of studies such as ours. Our thanks go also to a number of graduate students and their supervisors, Helene Kassen and Paul Perez, who during the summer of 1951, helped work out the ways of assessing the interview material that had not been precoded.

Our colleagues at the Research Center for Human Relations participated actively in the study and rendered valuable assistance in many ways. In particular we should like to thank Morton Deutsch, whose experience in the study of which this is in part a replication, proved of great value; Claire Selltiz, who assisted in the revision of the first draft of this report; and Isidor Chein, who read several sections critically and who helped in the preparation of Chapter XI. Marie Jahoda contributed greatly to the study at various stages: her ideas figured in the formulation of measures to determine the initial comparability of our respondents, she took an active part in revisions of the manuscript, and her irrepressible good spirits provided needed morale at low points in the conduct of the study.

During the course of the study we were fortunate in having a Technical Advisory Committee to act as guide, sounding board, and evaluator of the research at different points in its development. This Committee was headed by Professor Gordon W. Allport, Harvard University, as chairman, and consisted of the following persons in the field of housing, race relations, and social science: Elizabeth Wood, then Executive Director of the Chicago Housing Authority; Dr. B. T. McGraw, Deputy Assistant to the Administrator, Housing and Home Finance Agency; Dr. Channing Tobias, then Director of the Phelps-

Stokes Fund; Professors Otto Klineberg and Robert K. Merton, both of Columbia University. Members of the committee took time from busy schedules to help plan the study and review the final report. We are especially grateful to Professors Allport and Merton. Their critical ideas led to many worth-while revisions of the manuscript.

The preparation of various drafts of the manuscript was materially aided by the conscientious work of the secretarial staff of the Research Center for Human Relations. In this connection, we wish especially to thank Miss Jean Kawesch, Mrs. Dorothy Haas, and Miss Eleanor Walters.

Lucile Wilner painstakingly prepared the index.

The Marshall Field Foundation supplied the funds for this research, as it did for the research reported in *Interracial Housing* by Deutsch and Collins. Without the Foundation's continued assistance, this instance of *continuities* in social research could not have been undertaken.

Daniel M. Wilner and Rosabelle Price Walkley

FORMERLY AT THE RESEARCH CENTER FOR HUMAN RELATIONS,
NEW YORK UNIVERSITY; NOW AT THE SCHOOL OF HYGIENE AND
PUBLIC HEALTH, THE JOHNS HOPKINS UNIVERSITY

Stuart W. Cook

RESEARCH CENTER FOR HUMAN RELATIONS,
NEW YORK UNIVERSITY

May 1955

Contents

HUMAN RELATIONS
IN INTERRACIAL HOUSING

CHAPTER I

The Problem

Introduction

RECENT years have seen concerted effort in many quarters to reduce the tensions existing between antagonistic ethnic and religious groups. Much of this effort has been concentrated on the understanding and elimination of antagonisms between the Negro and white groups in the United States. The seriousness of problems of prejudice and discrimination needs no further comment here, nor does the urgency of finding effective solutions to these problems.

One of the solutions most frequently advocated as a step in the reduction of prejudice is the elimination of enforced segregation between Negroes and whites. This step is urged on two general grounds: First, enforced segregation involves injustice, both material and psychological, to Negroes. It cuts a majority of Negroes off from such fruits of technological society as personal advancement and economic security. Moreover, enforced segregation is held to be humiliating; it implies inferiority of present and potential social status; it creates frustrations and engenders mental ill-health; it is accompanied by disease and crime. Second, enforced segregation is also believed by many to have detrimental effects on the material and psychological life of the white majority. It is held to contribute to the psychological ill-health of white individuals by perpetuating a notable exception to the American creed; the contradictions thus engendered lead to guilt feelings and "various disturbances in the sense of reality" (4). Segregation is also thought to *reinforce* in many ways the prejudice—the stereotyped beliefs, the low regard, the distrust—that many white individuals have against Negroes.

Instances of elimination of segregation sometimes come about through efforts aimed directly at this goal. In other cases, desegregation has been a by-product of other activities aimed at improving the lot of the Negro minority rather than a goal in itself. For example, fair employment practice laws have as their primary goal the improvement

3

of economic conditions of Negroes through the opening of employment opportunities on equal terms. The hiring of Negroes on the same terms and in the same jobs as white workers leads to situations in which there is face-to-face contact between Negroes and whites, but this is a side effect rather than the primary purpose of such legislation. In still other instances, increased physical proximity between whites and Negroes comes about without explicit intention through the operation of impersonal social and economic processes, with neither the view to the improvement of the lot of the Negro nor to the amelioration of intergroup relations. The moving of Negroes into neighborhoods inhabited by white persons is a case in point.

Out of this variety of motives and causes has come a marked increase, within recent years, of situations in which Negroes and whites are brought into close physical proximity, with at least the possibility of contact and social interchange between individuals of the two groups on a basis of equality in terms of their defined roles within the proximity situation. Social scientists have taken advantage of such situations to carry out a number of studies. These studies have had a dual goal: to obtain information which will provide a useful guide for policy decisions and administrative procedures and to increase understanding of the dynamics of attitude change.

The present authors have reviewed some thirty studies, published and unpublished, bearing more or less directly on the effect that proximity between members of different ethnic groups has on intergroup attitudes.* A brief review of a number of these studies appears in the Appendix.

The cumulative evidence of these studies seems to provide rather substantial support for the general hypothesis that equal-status contact between members of initially antagonistic ethnic groups under circumstances not marked by competition for limited goods or by strong social disapproval of intergroup friendliness tends to result in favorable attitude change. Why this should be so requires a brief discussion of the nature of prejudice.

Ethnic prejudice may be thought of as a system of beliefs, feelings, and policy orientations regarding one or more ethnic groups.† Con-

---

* Most of these studies focused on the attitudes of white persons toward Negroes. For the most part, the effects of biracial proximity or contact on the attitudes of Negroes toward whites have not been investigated in detail—not because such effects were considered unimportant, but because of the general recognition that discrimination is primarily a problem of white people and that the elimination of prejudice and discrimination must be accomplished through the reorientation of the majority group. The present study follows this general orientation.

† See Deutsch and Collins (7), Chein (5), and M. B. Smith (23).

siderable evidence suggests that these beliefs, etc., are learned primarily from the communicated attitudes of members of one's own group, rather than on the basis of direct experience with members of the group against which prejudice is entertained.* The "typical" prejudiced attitude of white persons toward Negroes in the United States may be characterized as follows: Negroes are believed to be low-class, dirty, lazy, ignorant, etc.; the feelings accompanying these beliefs tend to be those of contempt, distrust, avoidance; policy orientations are in the direction of segregation and assignment of Negroes to positions of inferior status.

Existing social arrangements reinforce all these dimensions of prejudice. The fact that Negroes are, in practice, assigned to inferior positions and segregated from the white majority provides both support for the view that this is the *proper* social arrangement and, in a circular way, the basis for the assumption that this arrangement is based on the inferiority or undesirability of Negroes. Segregation operates to reinforce prejudice in still another way. By limiting the opportunities for interaction with individual Negroes (except in situations marked by clear status differences, as in the case of employer and domestic worker), it protects the white person from having to check his beliefs against reality.

Contact between the white majority and Negroes on a basis of equal status under certain relatively favorable circumstances tends to remove both these types of support for prejudice. If the contact is sanctioned by an individual or organization which carries authority and prestige (as, for example, an employer who hires whites and Negroes to work side by side at the same jobs, or a housing management which assigns Negroes and whites to apartments as neighbors), the assumption that segregation is right and inevitable is challenged. If the contact is sufficiently close to permit accurate observation of the personal characteristics of the Negroes in the situation, the white person is faced with the necessity of somehow reconciling the evidence from his own experience with his previously held stereotypes. Since any cross section of Negroes is likely to deviate considerably from the usual stereotypes, the perceived characteristics are likely to conflict with former beliefs. If strong personal motivations to retain prejudiced attitudes are absent, the importance of accepting the evidence of one's own senses as valid is likely to lead to a change in beliefs.† Moreover, if the contact experience is on the whole pleasant the feeling dimension of attitude may also be affected.

* See, for example, Horowitz (11).
† See Deutsch and Collins (7).

In this brief discussion, an attempt has been made to outline, in the broadest terms, the possible dynamics of changes in attitude resulting from equal-status contact between members of initially antagonistic groups. Many points, however, remain unclear—not only in terms of theory, but empirically as well. The following are among the points on which further information is needed: the relation between *proximity* and *contact*, and the relation of each to attitude change; the influence of initial attitude on the outcome of the contact experience; the influence of social pressures—or social climate regarding intergroup association—on the outcome of the contact experience, and the ways in which the social climate is established and manifested; the effect that different proportions of minority group members has on the experience associated with proximity or contact; and the dimensions of attitude which undergo change. The purpose of the present study has been to contribute to the understanding of the points just listed. Therefore, some elaboration of these issues seems desirable.

Relation between Proximity, Contact, and Attitude Change

Most investigators in this field have not distinguished sharply between proximity and contact. Some tacitly assumed that the degree of contact varies in direct proportion to the degree of proximity. Since we believe the distinction between the two concepts to be a necessary one, we shall throughout this report use "proximity" to refer to measurable physical closeness; while "contact" will be reserved for encounters in which there is mutual recognition and some sort of communication or social interchange between members of the two groups. It seems clear that it is possible for two groups to live in rather close proximity without any contact in this social sense. One of the crucial questions seems to us to be the relation between proximity and the occurrence of contact—or, more specifically, the conditions under which proximity leads to contact.

It may help in the understanding of the general problem if we examine the relationship of residential proximity to contact among persons of the same race. For individuals of the same race, the physical nearness of dwelling units is related to the likelihood of residents' meeting in face-to-face encounters, and to the establishment of social relationships between them. This is a proposition readily agreed upon when we consider extremes of distance. It seems clear that a resident of Chicago is more likely to encounter or make the acquaintance of a fellow Chicagoan than he is to meet someone who lives in Boston, a thousand miles away. Furthermore, several studies, involving persons of the same general ethnic groupings, have been reported showing the effects of fine gradations of distance. Kennedy (13), for example, found that in an eastern city, one-third of the marriages which took place within a year were between persons who had lived, at most, five blocks apart. In a recent study, Festinger, Schachter, and Back (9) report that the likelihood of face-to-face contact and establishment of social relationships is affected by differences in distance as small as twenty or thirty feet. In an all-white student housing project for married couples, residents in multiple-dwelling buildings (the buildings were two stories high with ten families per building) were asked which three families in the project they saw most of socially. In each building, 44 per cent or more of the choices made were of residents on the same floor. Moreover, the greatest proportion of mentions (as a percentage of possible mentions) was given to next-door neighbors, the next greatest to residents living an apartment away, and so on. The distance between the apartments at either end of a building was eighty-eight feet. The authors report similar findings relating distance units and social contact for a court in the project consisting of separate houses.

The following analysis may be made of the role of proximity in face-to-face contacts: Physical proximity leads to "functional" proximity, which involves the joint use of facilities necessary for access to one's apartment and for carrying out one's daily tasks; it means common stairways, sidewalks, laundry machines or sinks, and clothes lines; it means adjacent places to sit or stand while tending children. Such locations are likely to be the first meeting places of residents whose dwelling units are in close proximity. These first meetings may lead only to casual greetings. How the contact fares from then on is a function of psychological and other personal factors. The casual greeting stage may be enlarged, if the encounters are frequent enough and of sufficient duration, into acquaintanceships involving more or less extended conversations. Finally, if mutual interests are perceived and the individuals are compatible, these contacts may develop into friendships.

The housing project studied by Festinger, Schachter and Back was an extraordinarily homogeneous community with regard to age range of residents and general educational level and present occupation of at least the males in the households. It is difficult to estimate how much the homogeneity of the occupants of the project contributed to the development of friendships related, as indicated, to proximity. It may be supposed that this homogeneity made more likely the existence of "psychological and other personal factors" conducive to the development of casual encounters into more intimate acquaintance and friendship.

Now the question arises as to what occurs when persons in close proximity are of *different* races. The only investigators of interracial contact who seem to have considered explicitly the relation between proximity and contact are Merton, West, and Jahoda (17), and Deutsch and Collins (7).* Deutsch and Collins studied the white residents of two integrated and two area-segregated public housing projects; Merton, West, and Jahoda studied white residents of three terraces in a Negro-white public housing project—the terraces differing from one another in the proportions of Negro tenants present.

Both these studies found that proximity was related to the likelihood of Negro-white "friendships" or "neighborly activities." Deutsch and Collins asked their white respondents where they would be most likely to meet colored residents of the project. A majority of the respondents in the integrated projects mentioned the buildings in which they lived, or facilities near their buildings. On the other hand, a majority of the respondents in the area-segregated projects referred to the stores around the project as the most likely place to meet Negroes. It seems apparent that the chance encounters in and around the buildings would be more likely to provide opportunities for extended conversations than would those occurring in the stores.

These two studies suggest that, at least under the conditions existing in public housing projects, close Negro-white proximity results in a high probability of more than merely casual, passive encounters in much the same way that proximity leads to acquaintanceship and friendship in the all-white college project studied by Festinger, *et al.* In the integrated projects of Deutsch and Collins, and in the terraces of the Merton, West, and Jahoda project where large proportions of Negroes lived, physical proximity was associated with functional proximity which made certain face-to-face contacts between Negroes and whites almost impossible to avoid. For many of the white residents in these projects, the initial encounters developed beyond the superficial stages, evidently culminating in regular exchange of neighborly services and genuinely friendly relations.

Certain special circumstances in the settings of both studies may well have accelerated the development of Negro-white contacts. In all of the housing projects studied, the proportion of Negroes to whites was comparatively high—at least 40 per cent of the population in each project were Negroes—and this fact itself may have contributed to the incidence of contact. Moreover, a housing project is an entity readily distinguishable from the larger community, in which a social climate may arise which makes friendly interracial contacts at a more than superficial level *permissible* behavior, contrary to the social climate

---

* See fuller description of both studies in the Appendix.

regarding such contacts in the community at large. Furthermore, the fact that a public agency with prestige, such as the local housing authority, implicitly sanctions friendly relations by putting Negro and white families in the same or adjoining buildings is a situation not widely met elsewhere, and may provide support for the occurrence of friendly interracial contacts.

Influence of Initial Attitude*

Initial attitude may be thought of as a factor, directly or indirectly related to personality structure, which may be expected to influence the outcome of the contact experience. Few investigators have explicitly considered this point, beyond trying to insure that their comparison groups were originally similar in attitude. Those few investigators who have considered the reactions of initially more prejudiced and initially less prejudiced individuals within the contact group have come out with findings that are inconsistent with each other. Deutsch and Collins (7), estimating initial attitudes both on the basis of respondents' own reports and on the basis of a number of objective indicators known to be generally related to ethnic attitude, concluded that, in their integrated projects, persons initially unfavorable were *more* likely than those initially favorable to change in a favorable direction as a result of the experience of biracial living. (It must be remembered that statistically there was more opportunity for the initially unfavorable to move in a favorable direction.) On the other hand, Mussen (18), in a study of an interracial camp, found initial attitude not to be a significant determinant of change as a result of contact; the effect (if any) of initial attitude was overshadowed by that of personality variables.

---

* A good deal of evidence points to the conclusion that for some (perhaps many) individuals prejudice serves important personality needs, providing a sense of superiority to bolster a weak ego, offering an outlet for hostility which cannot be directed against its more appropriate object, etc. Adorno and his colleagues (2), Ackerman and Jahoda (1), and a number of other investigators working along somewhat similar lines have demonstrated rather clearly that there is a relation between character structure and the tendency to be prejudiced against ethnic groups other than one's own. These investigators have found that, at least at the extreme end of the scale, the prejudiced person tends to be an individual who is rigid, conventional, authority-oriented, with a good deal of repressed hostility. We know of only two studies which have explicitly considered the ways in which individuals with different types of character structure react to the experience of contact with minority group members. The first is that of Mussen (18) who studied boys attending an interracial camp for a period of one month and that of Dean (6) who studied the ethnic attitudes of a cross-section of white Protestant adults in two small northern cities. The findings of both studies seem to support the hypothesis that the effect of ethnic contact is different on persons with different personality organization, although it is not clear what personality "type" is affected in what way. The present study does not focus on personality measures directly. Instead, attention was given to the related concept of initial attitude, with its possible inhibiting or facilitating effect on the development of interracial contact.

Moreover, the relationship between initial attitude and personality variables was less strong than that between direction of attitude change and personality.

Not only the findings, but also the circumstances and the methods of these studies, were so different that it is impossible to draw any general conclusions from them. Clearly, the influence of personality structure and of initial attitude on change as a result of contact remains to be determined more precisely.

Influence of Social Climate

In our brief discussion earlier of the nature of prejudice, we stated that the prejudiced individual's attitude is given support by the existence of respected reference groups who are themselves prejudiced and by the existence of formal and informal restrictions against contacts with Negroes. What, if anything, happens to the influence of reference groups and institutions under conditions of residential proximity between the races? It may be, for example, that the experience of the white person in close proximity to Negroes provides sufficient disproof of stereotyped beliefs that the influence of reference groups on this issue is resisted. Where not merely individuals but whole groups of white persons are taking part in hitherto unaccustomed contacts with Negroes, still another possibility exists—the emergence of a group norm which supports the level and kind of Negro-white contacts that are likely to take place as a consequence of close proximity. It would be a finding of first importance to discover that, in a general atmosphere hostile to interracial contact, the very fact of close proximity between the races can give rise to counterpressures which sanction and increase the likelihood that such contacts will take place.

The emergence of a social climate compatible with the requirements of a group in reaching its goals has been described in many areas of investigation.* However, only in the Deutsch and Collins (7) and in the Merton, West, and Jahoda (17) studies has there been an attempt to measure systematically the perception of social atmosphere by the white participants in the interracial contact situation. Let us now examine in detail the findings of the Deutsch and Collins study on this issue. These authors entertained the hypothesis that a public housing project represented a sufficiently stable community in which evidence could be found of a group climate related to the individual's understanding of the total project situation. They therefore asked their respondents whether specified reference groups—the project management, other white housewives in the project, their friends outside the

* See, for example, Newcomb (19) and Festinger and Kelley (8).

project—would be likely to approve or disapprove of association with Negroes in the project.

They found that white respondents in the integrated projects differed systematically from those in the area-segregated projects in their anticipation of the reactions of various reference groups *within the project*. For example, the white housewife living in an integrated project was more likely than the one living in a segregated project to anticipate the approval of her friends in the project in the event that she was friendly with the colored people there. These authors stress that in the integrated projects they studied, unavoidable contacts were reinforced by the fact that the white resident knew that other housewives were having similar contacts; the very widespreadness of friendly Negro-white interaction within the project helped to remove some of the social barriers to further interaction. Further, Deutsch and Collins suggest that the physical arrangements—Negro and white families living in adjacent apartments—which were underwritten by a management policy admitting no exception helped to provide for many white tenants a reorientation regarding the social acceptability of close Negro-white proximity and interracial association.

White residents of the Deutsch and Collins area-segregated projects, on the other hand, knew from their daily observations that there was little face-to-face contact between Negroes and whites. Moreover, the occupancy pattern itself—clear-cut separation of the races into different areas—demonstrated continued sanction of this separation by an important social agency.

It remains to be determined what other specific conditions might contribute to the evocation of a social climate favorable to racial interaction. It may be that one's own contacts, "forced" by the necessity of comfortable existence and then found to be pleasant experiences, lead the individual to reject the disapproval of persons who have not had such contacts. Or it may be that certain special circumstances that accompany a large proportion of Negro participants in the contact situation—as in the integrated projects of the Deutsch and Collins study—aid the development of a climate favorable to interaction. These and other related matters are subjects for further research.

Effect of Different Proportions of Minority Group Members

On a priori grounds it seems probable that the proportion of Negroes to whites within the contact situation might have a bearing on the extent to which the white participants undergo attitude change. Little is known, however, about the direction of this effect; contradictory speculations seem equally tenable. The presence of only a few Negroes ("token integration") may not constitute sufficient demonstration of integration as an established social policy; moreover, it may be relatively easy to dismiss these few Negroes as "exceptions." With a greater proportion of Negroes, there is likely to be more occasion for white participants to have direct contact with Negroes. When the proportion of Negroes is very high, the white participants may feel threatened. Hogrefe, Selltiz, and Cook (21), interviewing group workers experienced in situations involving different ethnic groups, found for many of their informants that if the proportion of Negroes in a group exceeded a certain point—30 per cent was mentioned by several respondents—the white participants felt their presence as a threat and were likely to withdraw from the situation.

There has been almost no systematic investigation of the effects of varying proportions of minority group members in the contact situation, beyond that of Merton, West, and Jahoda (17), already reported, which found a direct relationship between the proportion of Negroes and the favorableness of white attitudes, even when Negroes constituted as much as 63 per cent of the population of an area. The great practical importance of this question points to the urgency of further research.

Dimensions of Attitude Undergoing Change

As noted earlier, intergroup prejudice is frequently considered to involve three dimensions: *beliefs* (indicating the common conceptions held by one ethnic group about the personal and social characteristics of another ethnic group), *feelings* (indicating the regard and esteem of one group for another group), and *policy orientation* (indicating the nature and extent of personal and institutional relationships to which one group is willing to admit another group). Kramer (14), Saenger and Flowerman (20), and Deutsch and Collins (7) have found that these dimensions are not uniformly affected by the experience of contact. The evidence suggests—though by no means conclusively—that beliefs may undergo change sooner than do feelings and policy orientation. There has been no investigation of the relation between specific factors in the contact situation and change in one or another dimension of attitude.

The present study has been designed to throw additional light on some of these points—in particular, on the relation between proximity, contact, and attitude, and on the effect of different proportions of minority group members. It has not been possible within this single study to secure data which would bear in detail on all of the points which still need investigation. The study is seen as one unit within the whole group of investigations which have focused on the hypothesis that equal-status contact between members of initially antagonistic ethnic groups leads to favorable attitude change. The general objectives of this group of investigations is to discover the conditions under which this relationship holds.

The Present Study

THE present study had as its general focus of investigation the effect of proximity between Negroes and whites—and certain concomitants of this proximity—on the attitudes of the white persons toward Negroes. Its aim was to throw additional light on some aspects of the problem which have not yet been thoroughly investigated. In particular, it was designed to parallel (and in one aspect to replicate) the study of Deutsch and Collins, with variations in specific factors which might have an important influence on the attitudinal outcome of the proximity experience.

Relation to the Deutsch and Collins Study

Deutsch and Collins, comparing white residents of four low-rent public housing projects, two of which were of integrated occupancy pattern and two area-segregated, found significant differences between residents of the two types of project on a number of indicators of behavior and attitude. The occupants of the integrated projects were considerably more likely than those living in the area-segregated projects to have neighborly interracial contacts, and to be more favorable on almost every measure of attitude.

The housing projects studied by Deutsch and Collins had, however, certain characteristics which might have been especially conducive to the favorable attitudes found in the integrated projects. This fact led to some question about how widely their findings with regard to the effects of occupancy pattern could be generalized. The present study was designed to test the generality of these findings by investigating the behavior and attitudes of residents of housing projects not marked by the special characteristics found in the Deutsch and Collins projects.

The two major factors that might have operated to enhance the effects of occupancy pattern were the high proportion of Negroes and the geographic location of the projects. In all four of the projects

14

studied by Deutsch and Collins, the proportion of Negroes was high, ranging from 40 per cent to 70 per cent of the total project population. All of the projects studied were in the metropolitan New York area; the integrated projects were located within New York City. Because of the possibility that the high proportion of Negroes and the unusually cosmopolitan composition of New York City might have been responsible for some of the effects attributed to occupancy pattern, the present investigation selected housing projects having a smaller proportion of Negroes and located in smaller cities away from the New York metropolitan area. The original intention was to study projects in which Negroes constituted about 25 per cent of the project population. It was not possible, however, to find suitable projects with the desired population proportions; of the projects finally selected, none had more than 10 per cent Negroes.* Two of the projects of the present study were located in middle-sized industrial cities (about 150,000 population) in New England; the other two were in larger cities (600,000 and 2,000,000 population) in a Middle Atlantic state at some distance from New York City.

Difficulties of locating comparable projects having the desired Negro-white proportions and geographic locations led to another important difference between the projects of the present study and those studied by Deutsch and Collins. The segregated projects of the earlier study had followed a pattern of area segregation, with white and Negro families in distinct sections of the project. The necessity of meeting the requirements of population proportion and geography in the present study led to the selection of two projects marked by a pattern of building-segregation. In these projects, although white and Negro families were assigned to separate buildings, the Negro-occupied buildings were interspersed throughout the project rather than concentrated in a separate section.

This difference between the segregated occupancy patterns of the projects in the two studies introduced some significant variations not originally intended. The possibility had to be considered that the building-segregated projects of the present study, although regarded by the investigators as segregated, may have represented to the occupants *less* segregation (or greater integration) than they had been accustomed to in the community at large. If this were so, the differences in attitudes between the occupants of these building-segregated proj-

---

* The problems encountered in locating housing projects in which such research could be carried on form in themselves a case study of considerable interest, illustrating both the difficulties inherent in the conduct of social research under field conditions and the relatively poor state of available information about occupancy pattern and other important aspects of public housing.

ects and the occupants of the matched integrated projects in the present study could not be expected to be as marked as the differences between the residents of the area-segregated and integrated projects of the Deutsch and Collins study.

While the original design of the present study stressed the comparison of the two kinds of projects, the combination of the low proportion of Negroes in all projects and the pattern of building-segregation in the segregated projects made possible investigation of the effects of Negro-white proximity independent of the effects of occupancy pattern per se. In the integrated projects of the Deutsch and Collins study, the high proportion of Negroes meant that almost every white family had a Negro family as a next-door neighbor, while in the segregated projects all white families were at some distance and clearly separated from the Negro families. In other words, all the white families in the integrated projects lived *close* to Negroes, while all white families in the segregated projects lived relatively *far* from Negroes. This concomitant variation made it impossible to investigate separately the effects of proximity and of occupancy pattern. In contrast, the low proportion of Negroes in the projects of the present study meant that even in the integrated projects relatively few white families had Negroes as next-door neighbors, while many white families lived in buildings where there were no Negroes. In the segregated projects, by reason of the presence of Negro-occupied buildings throughout the project, a considerable number of white families lived in buildings adjacent to, or in the same court with, a building housing Negro families. In both types of project of the present study, therefore, there were some white families who lived relatively *close* to Negroes and others who lived relatively *far* from any Negro family. Thus it was possible to compare white residents living at varying degrees of proximity to Negro families *within* projects of a given occupancy pattern (i.e., to investigate the effects of proximity with occupancy pattern held constant), as well as to compare projects of different occupancy pattern.

This combination of circumstances led also to the feasibility of a more detailed analysis of the interaction between face-to-face contact with Negroes and perceived social climate with regard to interracial association in contributing to attitude change. In the Deutsch and Collins study, a majority of the white women in the integrated projects had neighborly associations with Negroes and most of these women perceived their white friends in the project as approving such association, while in the area-segregated projects very few white women either had such associations or believed that other white women would approve of them. Since these two factors tended to vary concomitantly, it was impossible to distinguish their separate effects. In the present study, the small proportion of Negroes in all four projects, together with the less sharp separation of Negroes and whites in the segregated projects, suggested the possibility of considerably greater variation *within* projects both in the extent of contact and in the perception of a social climate regarding this contact, so that to some extent it seemed possible to distinguish these two factors and observe their interaction.

Description of the Projects

The present study was conducted in two public housing projects of integrated occupancy pattern and two of building-segregated pattern. Throughout this report these projects will be referred to as Integrated I and Integrated II, Building-Segregated I and Building-Segregated II. The Roman numerals stand for similarities as to the age of the project, size, rent, and geographic location. The numeral I symbolizes relatively new, relatively small, moderate-rental projects in middle-sized New England cities; the numeral II indicates older, larger, low-rental projects in larger Middle Atlantic cities. The four projects are described in greater detail in the following paragraphs.

Integrated I is located in a comparatively new section of a New England industrial city with a population of about 150,000. At the time of interviewing, there were 294 families in the project, of whom 29 were Negro. The project was completed and almost entirely occupied by November 1949. Integration was established at the beginning. In some dwelling units where a white family had moved out, a Negro family had been moved in; in one instance a white family had replaced a Negro family. About a quarter of a mile from the project is a very large, low-rental housing project containing 1000 families, of which 9 are Negro. Directly across one of the main thoroughfares which bounds Integrated I is an all-Negro project which is by no means as attractive in appearance or as well maintained as Integrated I.

Buildings are all apartment type, made of brick, two stories high, and are arranged in clusters, with three, four, or five buildings to a cluster. Some of the clusters are in a court pattern and some in a linear arrangement. In general, there is one Negro family in one of the buildings of each cluster. For the most part, there are four apartments to a building; a few have only two. Each of the four-apartment buildings has a common entrance for all the apartments. Dwelling units consist of three, four, or five rooms. The average rental is about $56 a month and does not include utilities.

The project was occupied entirely by World War II veterans and their families; thus there was considerable homogeneity in age. Ethnically, the project had very few Jews, a few Italians, and no nonwhites other than the Negro families.

At the time of the study, there was no tenants' organization. The project contains no central meeting place or community center. The project office staff consisted of the manager and his assistant, both white.

Building-Segregated I, the project with which Integrated I was matched, is located in the outskirts of another industrial New England city of about the same size (approximately 150,000), in an old but not deteriorated all-white residential neighborhood. At the time of the study, there were 200 families in the project, of whom 13 were Negro. Like its integrated "match," Building-Segregated I was completed and almost entirely occupied by November 1949. The building-segregated pattern was established from the beginning. The project is distant from other public housing developments in the city.

Most of the buildings are arranged in a distinctive court pattern. The Negro families live in four buildings scattered throughout the project. Dwelling units consist of three, four, five, or six-room apartments located in brick buildings one or two stories high. The four-room apartments are arranged four to a building, with a common entrance. The apartments of all other sizes are arranged either two, three, or four to a building, and each apartment has its own entrance. The average rental is about $40 a month but does not include utilities or oil for heat and hot water, the cost of oil averaging about $14 a month throughout the year.

The tenants were all World War II veterans, again making for a rather uniformly young population. As to ethnic composition, there were very few Jews living in the project at the time of the study, and no nonwhites other than the Negro families.

There was a tenants' organization, whose chief activity at the time of the study was to effect some changes in the rental system. The organization had both white and Negro membership.

The project had no central meeting place or community center. There was, at the time of the study, no project manager; the work of the former manager (white) was being done by two assistants, both white women. The office staff was not interracial, but the maintenance staff had one Negro.

Integrated II is located in a large Middle Atlantic city with a population of more than 2,000,000. The project is about half an hour's ride by public transportation from the downtown section of the city. It is situated in a predominantly white, lower middle class neighborhood. On one side, the project is bounded by an annex, with an all-white population, which has different architecture and in many ways is an independent project. Across a main thoroughfare on another side of the project is a temporary, all-Negro project, rather deteriorated in appearance.

At the time of the study, there were 991 families in the project, of which 88 were Negro. Integration was the stated policy from the time the project was opened in 1941, but at that time Negroes were placed in only one area of the project, leaving three other sections all white. In recent years, Negroes have been rented apartments in all sections of the project, but the original concentration had not yet been entirely altered. At the time of the study, the area where Negroes were first placed still had the greatest number of Negroes; in this section although there were now no all-Negro buildings, there were some buildings shared by Negroes *and* whites, and a few buildings in which only white families lived. In two other project areas, there were only a few buildings with Negroes in them, and then usually only one Negro family to a building. In a fourth area, there were no Negro families at all.

The buildings are two stories high, with from four to twelve apartments in a building. Each apartment has its own entrance, even those located on the second floor. Dwelling units consist of three to six rooms. The average rental is about $30 a month, with utilities included.

Although veterans of World War II were given preference, occupancy was not restricted to them; thus the age range was greater than in the moderate-rental projects. At the time of the study, there were a number of students and their families living in the project. Ethnic minorities consisted of a few Jews and less than ten families of such groups as Chinese, Japanese, and Puerto Ricans.

There was no tenants' organization at the time of the study, but in the center of the project is a large community building in which recreational and educational activities for adults and children were carried on, including a well-baby clinic. The office staff, all white, consisted of the project manager, his assistant, and an office force of three; there were Negro employees on the maintenance staff.

Building-Segregated II, the project with which Integrated II was matched, is located in an industrial Middle Atlantic city with a population of more than 600,000. It is in a suburb that is about thirty minutes by public transportation from the downtown section of the city. There is another housing project about a mile away. At the time of the study there were 448 families in the project, of whom 46 were Negro. The project was occupied in 1944 and had a pattern of building-segregation from the beginning.

About half of the project is located at the top of a steep hill, the other half at the bottom. Dwelling units consist of three to five rooms. There are from four to ten apartments in a building, each apartment having its own entrance. The buildings containing four apartments are one story high; all other buildings have two stories. The Negro families live in six buildings scattered throughout the project. The average rental is about $30 a month, including utilities.

As in Integrated II, although World War II veterans were given preference, occupancy was not restricted to them, and there was a considerable range in age of tenants. There were, at the time of the study, a few women who were separated or divorced from their husbands and who as heads of their households were living in the project with their children. The ethnic composition seemed to be similar to that of Integrated II.

On one of the boundaries of the project there is a community building which is the center of a fairly extensive activities program for children and teen-agers, but a considerably less extensive program for adults. A well-baby clinic was held in the building once a week. There was no tenants' organization.

Of the four projects studied, this was the only one with an interracial office staff. The project manager was white and his assistant was a Negro woman. There was at least one Negro on the maintenance staff.

Hypotheses

The present study was designed to test three sets of hypotheses: the first has to do with the relation between occupancy pattern and the dependent variables; the second has to do with the relation between proximity and the dependent variables; the third is concerned with the relation between contact, perceived social climate regarding contact, and attitude. Each set of hypotheses has already been touched on in the preceding chapter and in earlier sections of this chapter. At this point we shall enumerate the principal predictions, postponing the detailed rationale underlying each prediction as applied specifically to the four housing projects of the study.

OCCUPANCY PATTERN

1. Contact between white and Negro residents.

   Prediction: Relatively intimate contacts between whites and Negroes will be more likely to occur in the integrated projects than in the building-segregated projects.

   Measure: A series of detailed questions probing the nature of contacts undertaken with Negroes.

2. Perception of social climate with regard to interracial association.

Prediction: Residents of the projects with integrated occupancy pattern will tend to perceive a social climate more favorable to Negro-white association than will residents of the projects with building-segregated occupancy pattern.

Measure: Questions pertaining to the respondent's estimate of the reaction of her friends in the project and of management personnel toward friendly Negro-white interaction.

3. Attitude toward Negroes.

Prediction: White residents of the projects with integrated occupancy pattern will be more likely than residents of the building-segregated projects to accept the idea of Negroes and whites living together, to have favorable beliefs about, and feelings toward, Negroes in the project, and to have favorable attitudes toward Negroes in general.

Measure: A series of check-list and free-answer questions probing each of several dimensions of attitude.

PROXIMITY BETWEEN WHITES AND NEGROES *

4. Contact between white and Negro residents.

Prediction: White residents who live near Negroes will be more likely than those who live farther away to have relatively intimate contacts with Negroes in the project.

Measure: Same as for 1 above.

5. Perception of social climate with regard to interracial association.

Prediction: White residents who live relatively near Negroes will tend to perceive a social climate more favorable to Negro-white association than will those who live farther away.

Measure: Same as for 2 above.

6. Attitude toward Negroes.

Prediction: White residents who live relatively near Negroes will be more likely than will those who live farther away to accept the idea of Negroes and whites living together, to have favorable beliefs about, and feelings toward, Negroes in the project, and to have favorable attitudes toward Negroes in general.

Measure: Same as for 3 above.

LEVEL OF CONTACT, PERCEIVED SOCIAL CLIMATE, AND
ATTITUDE TOWARD NEGROES

7. The more intimate the contact, the more favorable will be the attitude; the more superficial the contact, the less favorable the attitude.

* While the original plan called for this analysis to be made in both the integrated and the building-segregated projects, it was expected that the predictions would be more likely to be supported in the integrated than in the building-segregated projects.

8. The more favorable the perceived social climate, the more favorable will be the attitude; the less favorable the perceived social climate, the less favorable the attitude.

9. Where relatively intimate contact coincides with favorable perceived social climate, attitude will tend to be *most* favorable. Where relatively superficial contact coincides with unfavorable perceived social climate, attitude will tend to be *least* favorable. Where the level of contact and the perceived social climate do *not* coincide, no prediction is offered.

Method

To obtain data for the purpose of testing our hypotheses, we conducted interviews with white tenants in the four housing projects. As in the Deutsch and Collins study, only *women* were interviewed, on the ground that factors connected with proximity and occupancy pattern are likely to have their greatest effect on housewives, who spend most of their day in the project.*

The present investigation used an ex post facto design. Since tenants were already living in the projects at the time the study was undertaken, it was impossible to obtain directly measures of the attitudes they held at the time they moved in. Instead, probable initial attitudes were estimated on the basis of a variety of other information. How this information was used will be described shortly.

As indicated by the hypotheses, two separate analyses were carried out: one was based on differences in occupancy pattern, the other on differences in proximity to Negroes. To test these hypotheses, the study of *one* integrated and *one* building-segregated project would perhaps have sufficed. However, confidence in the generality of results increases if the same process can be demonstrated to occur in different social settings and for this reason, primarily, the two pairs of projects were utilized.

Two kinds of samples of white respondents were constructed for the two basic analyses. Table 1 shows the size of the sample obtained for purposes of comparing projects of different occupancy pattern.

The sample in each project was selected so that it would be representative of groups of white tenants living at various degrees of distance from apartments of Negro residents. Thus, in Integrated I, 29 per cent of the white families in the project lived in the same building ("near") with at least one Negro family, and 71 per cent lived in all-white buildings ("far"); the sample for Integrated I contained "near" residents and "far" residents in this proportion.

---

* We do not intend the reader to infer that the results we report are uniform for men and women.

Table 1. Number of White Respondents and White Families
in Each Project

Project	Number of White Respondents	Total Number of White Families
Integrated I 150		265
Building-Segregated I 172		187
Integrated II 150		903
Building-Segregated II 135		402

Table 2. Percentage of "Nears" and "Fars" among White Residents in Each Project

Project	Total Number of White Families	Percentage of "Nears"	Percentage of "Fars"
Integrated I 265		29%	71%
Building-Segregated I 187		44	56
Integrated II 903		41	59
Building-Segregated II 402		21	79

Table 3. Number of "Near" and "Far" Respondents in Each Project

Project	Number of Respondents
Integrated I	
"Nears" (White housewives in buildings also housing one or more Negro families)	73
"Fars" (White housewives in all-white buildings)	107
Building-Segregated I	
"Nears" (White housewives in courts containing a Negro-occupied building)..	77
"Fars" (White housewives in all-white courts)	95
Integrated II	
"Nears" (White housewives in buildings also housing one or more Negro families)	113
"Fars" (White housewives in all-white buildings)	145
Building-Segregated II	
"Nears" (White housewives in buildings adjacent to a Negro-occupied building)	58
"Fars" (White housewives in buildings not adjacent to a Negro-occupied building)	138

Table 4. Number of Negro Respondents in Each Project

Project	Number of Negro Respondents	Total Number of Negro Families	Percentage Interviewed
Integrated I 25		29	86%
Building-Segregated I 13		13	100
Integrated II 67		88	76
Building-Segregated II 39		46	85

Table 2 shows the percentages of "near" and "far" residents actually living in each project.

For the purposes of comparing "nears" and "fars" the sample described above was not sufficient. The category "near" comprised too few cases to permit a detailed analysis. This category of residents was therefore sampled a second time with the aim of obtaining in every project approximately 75 "near" interviews. Table 3 shows the size and definition of the "near" and "far" groups thus obtained in every project.

As can be seen from Table 3, the definitions of "near" and "far" vary in accordance with the local circumstances. The proximity analysis uses by and large the dichotomy between near and far that is defined in Table 3. In a few instances finer degrees of proximity are distinguished.

The total "near"–"far" samples in Integrated II and Building-Segregated II contain only white residents who have lived in the project ten months or more at the time of interviewing. This selection was made because the effects of proximity to Negroes might not appear immediately but only after a period of living in such proximity. Comparable selection was not possible in the other pair of projects because such a limitation would have cut down too severely the possible number of respondents to be included in the sample.

Negro residents were also interviewed in each project, with the primary objective of obtaining information regarding their attitudes toward white residents of the projects. It was felt that the attitudes of the Negro residents could reasonably be expected to affect the changes in attitudes that we were seeking to measure among the white residents. Table 4 shows the number and proportion of Negroes interviewed in each project.

The interview schedule used in the present study was based on that of the Deutsch and Collins study, with some modifications to take account of the different circumstances in the projects of the present study, with other modifications to improve precision of measurement of certain variables, and with omission of a few items which had not proved fruitful in the earlier study. The present schedule covered the following general areas: the nature of the contacts taking place between whites and Negroes, perception of the social climate with respect to interracial association, beliefs about and feelings toward the Negroes living in the project, acceptance of the experience of interracial living, policy orientation with respect to occupancy pattern of future housing projects, attitudes toward Negroes in general, attitudes toward other minorities, and a number of background items used in estimating initial attitudes. The final interview schedule for white respondents consisted of eighty-six questions and took between one and a half hours and two hours to administer. A similar but shorter interview schedule was used with Negro respondents, certain inappropriate questions having been deleted.

The interviewing was done in the spring of 1951, beginning the last of March in Integrated I and concluding in Building-Segregated II in early June. Interviewing took from ten days to four weeks per project. Interviews were conducted primarily during the day, with at least three daytime call-backs at an apartment before calls were made in the evening. It was felt that daytime interviewing provided the best opportunity for an hour or two alone with the housewife. When a designated housewife refused to be interviewed or for some other reason was not available, another respondent was drawn from a substitute sample made up of white residents living an equivalent distance from Negro tenants. Total refusals did not exceed 8 per cent in the four projects.

The interviewers were given careful training in the use of the interview schedule. Although they were, of course, given an explanation of the general purpose of the research, *nothing was said about the intended analysis—the comparisons of integrated and segregated projects and of "nears" and "fars."* This reticence was essential in view of the possible conscious or unconscious biases that might have been introduced by overcooperative interviewers. An added safeguard against the effect of possible interviewer bias was the effort to have each interviewer collect data from white residents in different proximity-to-Negro designations, rather than interviewing only "nears" or only "fars."

The information from the interviews was coded and transferred to IBM cards. As with the interviewers, precaution was taken against possible biasing effects of overcooperation by the coders. Although the coders were aware of the nature of the planned analysis, information regarding the proximity category of the respondents was masked out and not known to them.

Coding itself was verified at every step. Qualitative codes were pretested on a sample of questionnaires for applicability and reliability. A qualitative code was considered satisfactory if two coders working independently agreed in 85 per cent of the cases. Refinements and reinterpretations of code categories were worked out on further pretest samples until the desired reliability was reached.

Statistical tests for significance of differences between groups have been made throughout this report. As a rule tables will report the statistic used and the significance level reached for each comparison. In some instances the statistic is the critical ratio, computed as

$$\frac{\text{Difference between proportions}}{\sigma_{\text{Difference between proportions}}}.$$

In most instances, the statistic used is the $2 \times n$ chi square (χ^2). In general the calculations of χ^2 and the degrees of freedom correspond to the number of categories presented in the tables. Where any categories contained frequencies too small to permit such calculation, they were combined with other categories and the probabilities were then estimated with fewer degrees of freedom.

Outline of Chapters

Since the major contribution of the present study is the investigation of the effects of Negro-white *proximity* as distinct from occupancy pattern, comparisons of white residents living at varying distances from Negroes will be presented first and in the greatest detail. These comparisons are given in Chapters III and IV. Chapter III discusses the relation between proximity, on the one hand, and, on the other, the extent of interracial contact and the perception of the prevailing social climate with regard to such contact. Chapter IV presents the relation between proximity and various dimensions of attitudes. In both of these chapters, comparisons between proximity groups are given, assuming, for the moment, that residents in the various proximity groups are initially comparable and thus that the differences between the groups can be attributed to the effects of proximity. Chapter V presents the data on which this assumption is based—estimates of the initial attitudes of "nears" and "fars." Chapter VI examines the relative influence of initial attitude and of proximity. Chapter VII considers the roles of contact and the perceived social climate in their direct relationship to attitude change. Chapters VIII and IX compare residents of projects of different occupancy pattern with respect to contact, perceived social climate, and attitudes. Chapter VIII presents *existing* differences between projects of the two occupancy patterns; Chapter IX discusses the initial comparability of tenants in the two types of projects and re-examines the observed differences in the light of these data. Chapter X compares certain findings of the present study with those of the Deutsch and Collins study, and Chapter XI presents a brief summary of all the findings of the present study.

CHAPTER III

Interracial Contact and Proximity

THE purpose of the present chapter is twofold. First, we wish to sketch the relationship between the physical distance separating whites and Negroes and the extent and nature of the contacts taking place between them. We shall rely principally on reports of white tenants concerning the kind of contacts they have with Negroes. Secondly, we wish to sketch the relationship between the distance separating the races and what the housewife sees as the social pressures to include or not to include the Negroes of her immediate surroundings in her everyday activities. Here our evidence will come principally from questions in the interview which asked the respondent how much Negro-white interaction she saw going on about her, and which asked for her inferences about the opinions of management and her friends toward such contact.

Contact between the Races in the Project

It has been observed both in everyday experience and in systematic investigations that contact, per se, between ethnic groups does not necessarily result in more favorable attitudes of one group toward another. However, review of research* suggests that contact under conditions of equal status *does* increase the likelihood of favorable effects on ethnic attitudes.

It is a basic assumption of the present study that such contact as occurs between Negroes and whites in public housing projects is equal-status in character. In this respect the public housing development is unlike many other meeting places between races. Similarity of socioeconomic class is guaranteed by income limits imposed by law on *all* occupants. Residents, Negro or white, are equally likely to have had severe housing need prior to moving in. Moreover, the project facilities are equally available to Negroes and whites alike: the apartments are

* See Chapter I and the Appendix.

similar, rentals are similar, management services are similar. These conditions are supplemented by the great similarity of family composition and of everyday activities of the Negro and white housewives. Whatever the race of the family, husbands must be got off to work, and children to school or ready for play; housework must be done and food prepared. When there are such great similarities among the tenants, whether Negro or white, there is little objective support for any feeling among white women, for instance, that they in some way have the better of it. Thus, when Negro women and white women meet —and we shall see shortly what the nature of the contact is—the encounters take place under conditions of equal status in the project community.

In connection with one of the hypotheses offered in Chapter II it was predicted that white residents who live near Negroes would be more likely than those who live farther away to have relatively intimate contacts with Negroes in the project. In presenting data bearing on this hypothesis, we shall first compare the "nears" and "fars" in each project. It will be remembered that in the two integrated projects, white women living in buildings which also housed one or more Negro families were considered to live "near" Negroes; white women living in all-white buildings were classified as living "far" from Negroes. In Building-Segregated I, with its court arrangement, white residents living in courts which include a Negro-occupied building are considered "nears," and are contrasted with white residents living in all-white courts ("fars"). In Building-Segregated II, which does not have a court arrangement, white residents living in buildings next to an all-Negro building are classified as "nears," and are contrasted with white residents who do *not* live in buildings adjacent to an all-Negro building ("fars"). These divisions within the four projects define the independent variable: proximity to Negroes within the project. The first question to be answered by the data is, How is interracial contact affected by proximity?

INDEX OF CONTACT

An attempt was made in the course of the interview to determine, for each white respondent, her characteristic level of interaction with Negro tenants in the project. The white respondent was asked* whether, in her chance encounters with Negro women in the project,

---

*Most of the questions asked in the course of the interview will be presented in the text, either in full or in paraphrased form, as the data on each question are described. Readers desiring a copy of the complete questionnaire may address the Research Center for Human Relations, New York University, Washington Square, New York, New York.

there was mutual greeting; whether during such encounters she stopped to talk; and whether she took part with Negro women in such neighborly activities as visiting back and forth, helping one another out in various ways (baby-sitting, etc.), doing things together (going shopping together, etc.). From the answers to these questions a "scale of interracial contact" was constructed, ranging from "no contact" whatsoever, at one end, to "participation in neighborly activities" at the other. In general, a respondent who stops to talk with Negroes in casual street encounters also greets them in the street. A respondent who takes part in neighborly interracial activity also greets Negroes and stops to talk to them in casual street encounters.

When we compare groups of respondents, in each of the projects, who have been distinguished from one another on the basis of their proximity to Negroes, we see some difference between the groups at every level on the scale.* The data for the four levels of contact are shown in Table 5.

No contact. A respondent was designated as having "no contact" if she reported no interaction with Negro residents, not even casual exchange of greeting when meeting them on the street or in a building. Table 5 shows that, in each of the projects, white housewives living relatively far from Negroes are more likely to report "no contact" than are those living closer. For example, in Integrated I, only 7 per cent of the white respondents who live in the same building with Negroes report "no contact" with Negroes in the project, compared to 23 per cent who live in all-white buildings. Similarly, in Building-Segregated I, only 8 per cent of the white respondents in the Negro-white courts report "no contact" with Negroes in the project, against 33 per cent in the all-white courts. For Integrated II and Building-Segregated II, Table 5 shows analogous findings.

Casual greeting. A number of respondents in the four projects reported that they exchanged greetings, but nothing more than that, in casual street encounters with Negro residents. Table 5 shows that white housewives living relatively far from Negroes are more likely than those living closer to report only such superficial contact. For example, in Integrated I, 15 per cent of the white respondents who live in Negro-white buildings report only "casual greeting," compared to 36 per cent of those who live in all-white buildings. The results are similar for two of the three other projects.

Combining these first two steps of the scale, we find that in each of

---

* In the comparisons of respondents within a given project, the reader may assume that all white residents were initially comparable in estimated attitude toward Negroes. That this is a reasonable assumption will be demonstrated in Chapter V.

Table 5. Relation between Proximity and Level of Contact of White Residents with Negro Residents

Level of Contact*	Integrated I		Building-Segregated I		Integrated II		Building-Segregated II	
	Near (73)†	Far (107)	Near (77)	Far (95)	Near (113)	Far (145)	Near (58)	Far (138)
No contact ..	7%	23%	8%	33%	12%	44%	2%	14%
Greets Negroes in casual street encounters ...	15	36	26	40	26	26	26	47
Stops to talk in casual street encounters with Negroes .	23	23	36	25	28	17	50	26
One or more kinds of neighborly activity‡.	[55]	[18]	[30]	[2]	[34]	[13]	[22]	[13]
1 kind only.	8	6	4	2	11	9	14	7
Any 2 kinds	17	7	9	...	11	2	5	2
All 3 kinds.	30	5	17	...	12	2	3	4
χ^2	31.9		39.0		41.2		19.0	
d.f.	3		3		3		3	
p	<.01		<.01		<.01		<.01	

*In general, a respondent who stops to talk with Negroes in casual street encounters also greets them in the street. A respondent who takes part in *neighborly* interracial activity also greets Negroes and stops to talk with them in casual street encounters.

†The figures in parentheses throughout this sequence of tables indicate the number of cases on which the percentages are based.

‡The bracketed figures represent the totals of the three figures below.

the four projects well over half (from 59 per cent to 73 per cent) of the respondents whom we have designated as living "far" from Negroes have no more than superficial interracial contact. On the other hand, this is true for proportions that range from 22 per cent to 38 per cent of those living "near" Negroes.

Stopping to talk and *neighborly activity*. The less superficial interracial contacts show, of course, the reverse trend. When we compare proximity groups within each of the four projects we find that "nears" are more likely than "fars" to report contacts of a more inclusive type. Combining the last two steps in the scale, it can be seen that, in the four projects, from 62 per cent to 78 per cent of respondents living relatively near to Negroes report *at least* stopping to talk with Negro residents in casual meetings, against a range of from 27 per cent to 41 per cent for those who live farther away.

Especially noteworthy is the contrast between groups in the proportions reporting the highest level of the scale, neighborly association with the other race. A white resident was said to participate in neighborly activities with Negro residents if she and any of the Negroes in the project customarily visited one another, did one of a number of things together, such as shopping, etc., or helped one another out in any of a number of ways. We find, in each of the four projects, that a greater proportion of white women who live near Negroes than of those living farther away report having one or more of the three kinds of interracial neighborly activities. In Integrated I, for example, 55 per cent of those living in mixed buildings have such contact, compared to only 18 per cent in all-white buildings. In Building-Segregated I the proportions are 30 per cent in the mixed courts to only 2 per cent in the all-white courts. Similar trends occur in the other two projects, although the differences are smaller.

Since the level of interracial contact appears, in all projects, to be so consistently related to proximity, it is desirable to explore this relationship still further. It will be remembered, from Chapter II, that it was possible to identify finer gradations of proximity in each project than those used in the basic "near-far" dichotomy presented in Table 5. In Integrated II, for example, it was possible to distinguish *four* subgroups according to proximity. Thus, among the 113 white respondents who live in the *mixed Negro-white buildings* (classified as "nears" in Table 5), 62 live in apartments directly next door to a Negro family, and 51 do not. Furthermore, of the 145 white respondents who live in the all-white buildings (classified as "fars" in Table 5), 70 live in areas where Negroes constitute less than 5 per cent of the population, and 75 live in completely white areas. In each of the three other projects it was possible to identify *three* proximity groupings; their locations are shown in the headings of Tables 6A and 6B.

It is clear from these tables that even when we consider the finer subdivisions of proximity, in all the projects there is a consistent trend relating proximity and contact: the nearer a respondent lives to Negroes—even on these refined scales of proximity—the more likely is she to report having contacts with Negroes that are more than superficial.

It is thus clear, assuming that respondents living various distances from Negroes within a project were truly comparable when they moved in, that proximity itself makes an enormous difference in how well whites and Negroes are going to know one another. It is important to note that the relationship between proximity and extent of contact holds even in the segregated projects, where those who live "near" Negroes are, at closest, in an adjacent building.

Table 6A. Relation between a Finer Degree of Proximity and the Level of Contact of White Residents with Negro Residents—Moderate-Rental Projects

	Integrated I			Building-Segregated I		
	Near (Negro-White Bldg.)		Far	Near (Negro-White Court)		Far
Level of Contact	Next Door to Negro Family (29)	Not Next Door to Negro Family (44)	All-White Building (107)	Building Next to Negro Building (33)	Building Not Next to Negro Building (44)	All-White Court (95)
No contact	7%	7%	23%	3%	11%	33%
Greets Negroes in casual street encounters	14	16	36	21	30	40
Stops to talk in casual street encounters with Negroes	14	29	23	37	37	25
One or more kinds of neighborly activity ...	65	48	18	39	22	2
χ²		36.0			44.0	
d.f.		6			6	
p		<.01			<.01	

Table 6B. Relation between a Finer Degree of Proximity and the Level of Contact of White Residents with Negro Residents—Low-Rental Projects

	Integrated II				Building-Segregated II		
	Near (Negro-White Building)		Far (All-White Building)		Near	Far (Bldg. Not Next to Negro Bldg.)	
Level of Contact	Next Door to Negro Family (62)	Not Next Door to Negro Family (51)	In Negro-White Area (70)	In All-White Area (75)	Bldg. Next to Negro Bldg. (58)	In Negro-White Area (74)	In Mostly All-White Area (64)
No contact	11%	12%	37%	53%	2%	8%	20%
Greets Negroes in casual street encounters	25	27	29	23	26	45	48
Stops to talk in casual street encounters with Negroes	18	41	17	16	50	27	25
One or more kinds of neighborly activity	46	20	17	8	22	20	7
χ²		62.0				28.3	
d.f.		9				6	
p		<.01				<.01	

The results of the interviews with Negro housewives, all of whom, of course, live near white families in the project, showed that no fewer than half in any project had one or more kinds of neighborly association with white housewives in the project, and no fewer than four out of five had at least conversational contacts. Only 3 Negro housewives out of the 145 interviewed in all projects reported having no contact whatsoever with whites. These findings provide corroborative evidence of the white respondents' reports of interracial contacts in the projects. In fact, the proportion of Negro respondents reporting contacts with whites is greater than the proportion of whites reporting contacts with Negroes, as we would expect. This is due, in part, to the high proportion of white families in the projects. We know from the preceding tables which groups of white residents the Negroes had contacts with: although some of the contacts occurred with whites living relatively far from the Negroes, more were with whites living close by.

BACKGROUND OF CONTACT

Let us now examine some of the ways in which relative nearness of whites to Negroes increases the likelihood of interracial contact. White residents in the four projects were asked, "Where do you ordinarily see or run into the colored people who live here?" Table 7 illustrates strikingly that close proximity makes for repeated chance encounters in settings which are conducive to the development of further acquaintance—a finding which corresponds to that of Festinger, Schachter, and Back in their study of an all-white project mentioned in Chapter I.

The table shows the places where unplanned encounters are more likely to occur if the white resident lives relatively near Negroes than if she lives farther away. These places of encounter are "at the clothesline," "in project parking areas," "just outside your building," "in the stairway of your building," and "in someone else's apartment." In Integrated I, for example, white residents who live in mixed buildings are much more likely (84 per cent) to meet Negroes at the clothesline than are whites who live in all-white buildings (50 per cent). For the parking areas the proportions are 71 per cent to 50 per cent; just outside the building, 95 per cent to 88 per cent; in the stairway of the building, 82 per cent to 8 per cent; and in someone else's apartment, 34 per cent to 18 per cent. The figures for the other three projects are analogous.

Table 7 also shows that there are types of unplanned encounters with Negroes which almost every white respondent in the project is likely to have, regardless of the distance of her apartment from a Negro-occupied one. Thus, "nears" and "fars" are about equally likely

Table 7. Relation between Proximity and Likelihood of Unplanned Encounters with Negroes

Places	Integrated I		Building-Segregated I		Integrated II		Building-Segregated II	
	Near (73)	Far (107)	Near (77)	Far (95)	Near (113)	Far (145)	Near (58)	Far (138)
Places of Unplanned Encounters Related, in General, to Proximity to Negroes								
At the clothesline	84%	50%*	40%	7%*	71%	32%*	12%	4%
In project parking areas	71	50*	57	9*	57	29*	45	34
Just outside the building ...	95	88	87	47*	95	82*	72	51*
In the stairway of the building	82	8*	8	4	(no common stairways)		(no common stairways)	
In someone else's apartment.	34	18*	22	3*	16	5*	7	7
Places of Unplanned Encounters Relatively Unrelated to Proximity to Negroes								
In the streets of the project	81%	81%	90%	81%	96%	90%	91%	75%*
Waiting for a bus	93	91	67	73	95	92	93	96
At the project office	37	41	51	42	80	81	72	81

*Differences are significant at least at the .05 level of confidence as calculated by the t test for significance of differences between percentages.

to encounter Negroes in the streets of the project, generally while waiting for a bus, or in the project office. These places are relatively unrelated to the location of the apartments of either Negroes or whites. Such encounters, however, are not likely to involve the same individuals over and over; thus the likelihood of mutual recognition is slight. And unless prior acquaintance has been established, such encounters are likely to be fleeting, with little opportunity for more than the most casual conversation.

It appears, then, that those who live near Negroes are more likely to have interracial encounters under conditions conducive to further acquaintance. In the parking area, at the clothesline, on the stairs, and in someone else's apartment, contacts may be assumed to occur with considerable frequency and regularity; moreover, encounters in such settings are not necessarily of brief duration, but provide opportunity for conversation more extensive than mere greeting. On the other hand, for white residents living relatively far from Negroes there are lacking, under ordinary circumstances, the prime condition that makes for the development of more than mere recognition among the persons involved: namely, the realistic possibility of recurring meetings with the same persons under circumstances conducive to conversation and to the discovery and development of common interests.

Living near Negroes, however, does more than merely increase the likelihood of the relatively unplanned conversational contacts. It also makes more likely neighborly contacts centering around certain necessary home activities. Thus, among the diverse interactions which constitute "neighborly activities" reported in Table 5, the items which distinguished best between proximity groups were borrowing and lending, helping during sickness, minding one another's children, helping with shopping, and social visiting. In Integrated I, for example, a far greater proportion of the white housewives who live in mixed buildings than of those in the all-white buildings report each of these home-centered neighborly activities. For instance, 26 per cent in the mixed buildings, as compared with 3 per cent in the all-white buildings, report having coffee and tea together; 40 per cent in the mixed buildings, as compared with 8 per cent in the all-white buildings, report borrowing and lending. In the other three projects as well, these items show consistent differences between white housewives who live near Negroes and those who live farther away, although in the other projects the differences are, in general, smaller than those found in Integrated I.

In other words, living relatively near to Negroes makes it more likely that the white tenant will engage in such activities with Negroes as are necessary for comfortable living in the project. People who live near one another help one another in a variety of ways, practically and socially. Our data show that this occurs even when the persons who live near one another are not of the same race. As one white housewife who lived next door to a Negro family in Integrated II reported: "When my husband was ill, the [Negro] girl next door was wonderful— sent in food and gave me money." Another white respondent who lived in the same court with a Negro family in Building-Segregated I commented: "At first when we moved in I would hear people say, 'What are colored doing here?' Now I see them running back and forth. We all sit out and visit in the summer regardless of color."

What do white and Negro women talk about in the course of their conversations? An indication of the content of the conversations that involve more than mere greeting is provided by the answers (given in a check list) to the question: "What do you and the colored women in the project talk about when you talk?" It appears, as can be seen in

Table 8. Relation between Proximity and the Variety of the Topics Discussed in Interracial Conversation

Topic of Conversation	Integrated I		Building-Segregated I		Integrated II		Building-Segregated II	
	Near (73)	Far (107)	Near (77)	Far (95)	Near (113)	Far (145)	Near (58)	Far (138)
Schools	30%	11% *	27%	4% *	32%	6% *	41%	26%
Children	71	39 *	59	26 *	53	20 *	47	30 *
Husbands	45	12 *	30	5 *	19	6 *	2	7
Prices	63	22 *	38	16 *	42	14 *	41	25 *
The project	58	24 *	42	15 *	35	10 *	31	19
Laundry facilities.	26	7 *	12	3 *	13	6	9	4
Movies	30	7 *	19	6 *	14	4 *	9	4
Women in the project	29	7 *	19	7	12	5	3	4
War and other news	48	18 *	30	10 *	32	14 *	19	15
How colored and white get along..	26	7 *	22	...	15	3 *	5	4

*Differences are significant at least at the .05 level of confidence as calculated by the *t* test for significance of differences between percentages.

Table 8, that white and Negro housewives discuss every kind of topic imaginable: the war in Korea, husbands, other women, the project, the Negro-white problem, children, schools, etc.—in other words, the sort of list to be expected had the question been asked about conversations between members of the same race.

This is in line with our earlier finding regarding the different proportions of white women who, depending upon proximity to Negroes, engage in conversation with them. Now we find that a far greater proportion of white women living near Negroes than of those living farther away report discussing almost all the topics listed. Every topic in the list is more likely to be discussed with Negroes by women who live near than by those who live farther away. Thus, to mention a few characteristic examples, we find that in Integrated I, 71 per cent who live in mixed buildings report talking about their children with Negro women, compared to 39 per cent in the all-white buildings; interracial

Table 9. Relation between Proximity and the Extent of Visiting between White and Negro Children

Visiting among Children	Integrated I		Building-Segregated I		Integrated II		Building-Segregated II	
	Near (73)	Far (107)	Near (77)	Far (95)	Near (113)	Far (145)	Near (58)	Far (138)
Respondent's children going to Negro children's homes to play								
Yes	32%	10% *	27%	11% *	25%	10% *	14%	9%
No	42	74	67	85	56	71	86	84
No children, or children under two years	26	15	5	3	17	16	...	3
No answer		1	1	1	2	3	...	4
Negro children coming to respondent's home to play								
Yes	36	12 *	27	12 *	24	13 *	17	13
No	38	72	67	84	57	68	83	81
No children, or children under two years	26	15	5	3	17	16	...	3
No answer		1	1	1	2	3	...	3

* Differences are significant at least at the .05 level of confidence as calculated by the *t* test for significance of difference between percentages.

conversations include husbands as topics for 45 per cent of white respondents in mixed buildings, compared to 12 per cent in all-white buildings. When the topic is the project itself, the proportions are 58 per cent to 24 per cent respectively in mixed and all-white buildings; when it concerns how colored and white residents get along, the proportions are 26 per cent and 7 per cent. Similar differences appear on almost every item in the three other projects as well.

Table 9 gives information about another aspect of interracial contact. It would be surprising if the different levels of interracial contact taking place as a function of distance from Negroes were not reflected in the extent of contact between Negro and white children. One measure of the degree of interaction among the children of the two races is the extent to which they play in one another's homes. Respondents in the four projects were asked: "Do your children ever go into colored children's homes to play?" and "Do colored children ever come into your home to play?" As with the data for home-centered contacts among adults, the answers to these questions differentiate those who live close to Negroes in *each* of our projects from those who live relatively far away. For instance, in Integrated I, 32 per cent of white respondents who live in the mixed buildings report that their offspring visit Negro homes, compared to only 10 per cent of the respondents in all-white buildings. Similarly, 36 per cent in mixed buildings, and 12 per cent in all-white buildings, report Negro children as visitors in *their* homes. Similar statistically significant differences occur in two of the other three projects.

The detailed picture of the interracial contacts taking place within each of the projects has done much to confirm our hypothesis about the relation between proximity and the nature and extent of interpersonal contacts, even when the persons living near each other are not of the same race. Furthermore, the account of the circumstances surrounding the contacts and the nature of the topics discussed in interracial conversations support the supposition set forth earlier that the contacts represent equal-status interaction between Negroes and whites. It remains to be seen whether these interracial contacts result in the hypothesized alteration in ethnic attitude. This question will be discussed in detail in later chapters.

EXPERIENCES WITH NEGROES PLEASANT OR UNPLEASANT

The data presented so far indicate the extent and something of the content of contacts taking place between white and Negro tenants in the projects. They provide no direct evidence, however, about the feeling tone which characterizes the contacts. It seems hardly likely, when conversational and neighborly contacts take place between white and Negro residents, that they take place in a reserved and formal way without some warmth or friendliness about them. The great variety of topics of conversation with Negroes reported by white respondents living near Negroes, the conditions under which the contacts take place, the involvement of children, etc., all suggest that these contacts are essentially amiable.

In order to get more direct evidence about the feeling tone characterizing interracial contacts, the white respondents were asked whether their experiences with Negroes in the project had been pleasant or unpleasant. As shown in Table 10 a large number of women in each of

Table 10. Relation between Proximity and Evaluation of Experiences with Negroes in
the Project as Pleasant or Unpleasant

	Integrated I		Building-Segregated I		Integrated II		Building-Segregated II	
Evaluation	Near (73)	Far (107)	Near (77)	Far (95)	Near (113)	Far (145)	Near (58)	Far (138)
Pleasant experiences only	36%	18%	25%	12%	32%	18%	28%	25%
Pleasant and unpleasant experiences	12	4	...	2	8	4	10	6
Unpleasant experiences only	10	11	5	2	14	10	17	12
No pleasant or unpleasant experiences	42	67	70	83	46	68	45	57
No answer	...	...	...	1	...	...	...	...
χ^2	14.8		5.4		13.7		3.2	
d.f.	3		2		3		3	
p	<.01		<.10		<.01		>.10	

the projects replied that their experiences had been neither notably
pleasant nor notably unpleasant. The proportions giving this reply
ranged from 42 per cent to 70 per cent of respondents living near
Negroes, and from 57 per cent to 83 per cent of those living farther
away. These high proportions reporting essentially neutral or matter-
of-fact experiences with Negroes correspond closely to the proportions
in each project reporting contact less intimate than that involved in
neighborly activities.

When we examine the replies of those who report some affect in their
contacts with Negroes, it appears that the contacts are mostly pleasant
ones but, as in all interpersonal relations, there are some unpleasant
contacts as well. As might be expected from the greater frequency of
more than superficial contacts on the part of those living near Negroes
than on the part of those living farther away, the "nears" were more
likely to report having had interracial experiences marked by feeling
tone of *some* sort: pleasant, unpleasant, or mixed. If we combine
"pleasant experiences only" and "pleasant and unpleasant experiences"
to give the total of respondents who report *some* pleasant experiences
with Negroes in the project, we find that in every project white respondents living near Negroes were more likely than those living farther away to report having had *some* pleasant experiences. For example, in Integrated I, 48 per cent of the white respondents living in
mixed Negro-white buildings reported *some* pleasant experiences, com-

pared to 22 per cent of those in all-white buildings. The smallest difference between proximity groups in the proportions reporting *some* pleasant experiences was found in Building-Segregated II.

Moreover, it will be noted from Table 10 that in three of the four projects—Integrated I, Building-Segregated I, and Integrated II— white respondents living near Negroes were more likely than those living farther away to report having had *exclusively* pleasant experiences with the Negroes in the project. For example, a white respondent in Integrated I reported that the Negro woman who was her next-door neighbor "came over to keep me company when my husband was away. She's just swell." And another white housewife in the same project said that pleasant experiences with Negroes in the project derived from the pleasure of visiting with them in her own home and in the Negroes' homes. She said, "I have helped the [Negro] woman here [next door] out just as I would a white person."

Social Climate regarding Contact with Negroes

With prejudice as widespread as it is, it is the rare white resident who is not aware that many in our society would not approve of the interracial contacts taking place in the project. Everyone in the project is likely to be touched in some way by social pressures deterring friendliness with Negroes. And these pressures from outside the project act most probably in the same direction for all white residents, whether they live near to Negroes or relatively far from them.*

On the other hand, as one of our hypotheses suggested, it may well be that living in a project where there are Negro and white tenants gives rise to special social pressures centered in the project itself, which may be different from those in the larger community and which may operate differently depending on proximity to Negroes in the project. It is the purpose of this section to describe these pressures and the way they are related to the proximity of whites to Negroes in the project.

We shall discuss three project-centered sources of inference regarding the social permissibility of Negro-white association in the project. The first is the white resident's observation of the interaction of *other* white residents with Negroes in the project, the second is the anticipated reaction of friends in the project to the respondent's associating with Negroes, and the third is the respondent's interpretation of the intentions of the officials responsible for the Negro-white arrangements in the project.

---

*For example, data to be given in Chapter V with regard to the estimated initial attitudes of white residents show that the opinions of friends and relatives outside the project are likely to be negative toward the idea of the respondents' living in a biracial project, whether the respondents live near to or far from Negroes in the project.

PERCEPTION OF CONTACT BETWEEN WHITE AND NEGRO RESIDENTS

One indication of the acceptability of certain behavior is the direct perception of how others in one's environment are acting in similar situations. In order to keep up with the Joneses, one must know how the Joneses are behaving.

A question was asked in the interview regarding the actual mingling the respondent observed taking place between Negroes and other white women in the project. In all four projects white residents living relatively near Negroes are more likely than those living farther away to report that whites interact with Negroes in about the same way that whites interact with other whites. For example, one white respondent who lived near Negroes in Integrated II said: "Everyone is friendly with them [the Negroes in the project]. They [the whites] dance with them at the dances." On the other hand, a white respondent in the all-white area in the same project commented, "You never see them [the whites] mingle with the Negroes."

In Building-Segregated I and Integrated II the differences between "nears" and "fars" are substantial. For example, 40 per cent of the white respondents living in mixed courts in Building-Segregated I report white women mingling with Negro women "the way they do with white women," while only 18 per cent of those living in all-white courts report this perception of Negro-white interaction. In Integrated II, 47 per cent of respondents who live in the same building with Negroes report that white women mingle with Negro women the way they do with white women, as compared to 24 per cent of those who live in all-white buildings. In Integrated I and Building-Segregated II the differences between the proximity groups are less substantial but show a trend in the same direction. In Integrated I the difference between "nears" and "fars" in the percentage reporting whites mingling with Negroes in about the same way as they do with whites is 9 per cent; in Building-Segregated II the difference is 8 per cent.*

Material presented earlier in this chapter provides insight into some of the primary sources of these differences. There was a substantial

---

* A word is in order about the relatively small differences between proximity groups in Integrated I and in Building-Segregated II. In Integrated I, it will be recalled, the distribution of Negroes is such that, in general, a single Negro family lives in one of a small cluster of buildings, and there are no all-white areas. Thus one is very likely to observe roughly the same kind of street interaction between the races whether one lives in a mixed building or an all-white building. As a consequence we might expect smaller proximity-group differences in reports of perception of interracial contact. In Building-Segregated II, on the other hand, the proportion of respondents in the project *as a whole* who report interracial encounters *near* one's building is smaller than in any other project. Under these circumstances a reduction in differences between proximity groups in the proportion reporting observation of Negro-white interaction might be anticipated.

difference between proximity groups within each project in the proportions of white residents who engaged in conversations with Negro residents or who participated in neighborly activities with them. It will be remembered that many of the chance interracial encounters which led to conversations took place in the streets or other public areas of the project, especially in the vicinity of the respondent's own building. It is reasonable to assume that such meetings are observed by *other white women* in the project. Moreover, it is equally reasonable to suppose that the white women most likely to observe such interracial contacts are those who themselves live relatively near to Negroes, since these contacts are most likely to occur in areas where Negroes live.

With regard to the more neighborly activities, it will be recalled that in three of the four projects white tenants living near Negroes were more likely than those living farther away to report meeting a Negro resident in someone else's apartment. This leads to the further supposition that a white person living near a Negro family is more likely to observe home-centered neighborly contacts between the races than is one who lives farther away.

In other words, it appears that the very circumstances which make it more likely that those living near Negroes will have frequent chance encounters with Negroes and perhaps enter into relatively intimate association with them also make it more likely that these various interracial contacts will be observed by white residents who live near Negroes.

ANTICIPATED REACTIONS OF FRIENDS IN THE PROJECT

The wish to maintain the favor of one's friends is an important determinant of one's behavior. If a white resident realized that her friends and acquaintances in the project were hostile to Negroes, this realization might play a role in keeping her from expanding her own contacts with Negroes. On the other hand, if it was clear to her that her friends in the project were not hostile to Negroes nor to the idea of being friendly with Negroes, this might well remove an impediment to enlarging such contacts. The summary inference that a person draws regarding the probable reactions of others to certain behavior may arise from several sources. One source in the case of Negro-white interaction may be direct communications among white women in the project. Another we have already mentioned: the white resident's direct observation of the extent to which other white women associate with Negroes in the project.

It might be expected, therefore, that there would be differences in the respondents' interpretation of the *feelings* of their friends in the project regarding this issue, depending upon how close to Negroes they

Table 11. Relation between Proximity and Perception of the Social Climate

Anticipated Reaction of White Friends to Friendly Association with Negroes	Integrated I		Building-Segregated I		Integrated II		Building-Segregated II	
	Near (73)	Far (107)	Near (77)	Far (95)	Near (113)	Far (145)	Near (58)	Far (138)
Generally favorable	58%	49%	51%	24%	46%	25%	31%	24%
Mixed	5	3	3	7	3	2	5	2
Generally unfavorable	23	33	30	36	31	55	58	59
Don't know, not classifiable	14	15	16	33	20	18	6	15
χ^2	1.2		14.0		16.0		2.7	
d.f.	2		2		2		2	
p	>.10		<.01		<.01		>.10	

live. White residents were asked: "How do your friends in the project feel about the idea of your being friendly with a colored family in the project?" The replies are shown in Table 11. In all four projects there is evidence that a white woman living near Negroes is more likely than one living farther away to believe that friends in the project approve (or would approve) of her friendly relations with Negroes. The differences between proximity groups are substantial in two projects. In Building-Segregated I, 27 per cent more among respondents living in mixed courts than among those in all-white courts feel that their friends are favorable to the idea of friendly association with Negroes; in Integrated II, 21 per cent more among respondents who live in mixed buildings than in all-white buildings feel that their friends are favorable to the idea. In Integrated I and Building-Segregated II, the differences are in the same direction, but smaller; the differences between proximity groups within the project for the category "friends generally favorable to idea" are 9 per cent in Integrated I and 7 per cent in Building-Segregated II.*

The different kind of social climate perceived by "nears" and by "fars" may be illustrated by the following interview responses. A white housewife living in the all-white area of Integrated II said: "People I know would not like it [my being friendly with Negroes]. They don't get friendly with the colored." Another white respondent in the same all-white area put it even more strongly: "My one friend flies off the

---

* The reasons for the smaller differences in these projects are very likely the same as those offered for the relatively small differences between proximity groups in the same projects in the reports of perceived Negro-white interaction.

handle if you even mention them [the Negroes]." On the other hand, a white respondent in a mixed court in Building-Segregated I commented: "They [white friends] are just as friendly as I am to colored. We all feel the same way about it. We feel they are true friends."

The consistent trends in the responses just cited show that differences in proximity indeed bring with them not only differences in the extent of interracial contact, but also consistent differences in the respondents' impressions of the acceptability of such contact *in the eyes of the other tenants.*

The relationship between interracial contact and the social climate regarding that contact is an intimate one. From the day the white housewife moves into the project she is likely, if she lives near Negroes in the project, to find herself having contact of some sort with them. Her own experiences are paralleled by what she sees other white women doing and by what she infers their reactions would be to her behavior. For example, a white housewife living in a mixed court in Building-Segregated I said that her white friends in the project would feel "all right" about the idea of her being friendly with a Negro family in the project "because my white friend and I go to see their television," and another commented that some of her white friends ". . . have colored families in to watch television, so why should they mind?"

All interracial contacts, like associations between persons of the same race, are likely at first to be superficial. The white resident who lives near Negroes, and for whom the possibility of further contact is real, may find reinforcement for her own interaction with Negroes by observing similar contacts made by other whites near by. It is by a slow and cumulative process that one's own actions and the understanding of how those actions will be received by respected members of the community are integrated and result in final behavior tendencies.

INTERPRETING INTENTIONS OF MANAGEMENT

No action undertaken by the management of a housing project is likely to escape interpretation by the persons whom it affects. Therefore it was expected that management's policy regarding race relations (perhaps mainly reflected in the specific occupancy patterns) and the *behavior* of the management staff with regard to Negro-white interaction might be influential factors in establishing the social climate with respect to such interaction. To arrive at an estimate of this influence, two questions were asked of our respondents.

The first asked respondents in the integrated projects to account for the housing planners' putting Negroes and whites in the *same* buildings, and in the building-segregated projects to account for the housing planners' putting Negroes and whites in *separate* buildings. These questions will be discussed in detail in Chapter VIII, where the projects of different occupancy pattern are compared. It is sufficient to note here that *within* projects there are no appreciable differences in point of view between "nears" and "fars."

Table 12. Relation between Proximity and the Interpretation of Management's Attitude toward Friendly Negro-White Association

Reported Attitude of Management	Integrated I		Building-Segregated I		Integrated II		Building-Segregated II	
	Near (73)	Far (107)	Near (77)	Far (95)	Near (113)	Far (145)	Near (58)	Far (138)
Unqualified approval	49%	40%	36%	43%	48%	37%	46%	51%
Neutral, indifferent, or mixed	15	24	32	26	13	18	16	18
Unqualified disapproval	5	12	1	4	5	10	3	7
Don't know, not classifiable	31	24	31	27	34	35	35	24
χ^2	5.4		1.0		5.0		2.1	
d.f.	3		2		3		2	
p	>.10		>.10		>.10		>.10	

The second question asked what "the manager and those in the office think about whites and colored being friendly with one another." Table 12 gives the classification of the answers to this question. In general, there seems to be little relationship between proximity to Negroes within a project and the proportions reporting that management gives wholehearted approval or disapproval to friendly white-Negro interaction. Only in the integrated projects is there a tendency for respondents living near Negroes to be more likely than those living farther away to view management's attitude as favorable. In Integrated I, 49 per cent of the white respondents who live in mixed buildings report management's unqualified approval, as compared with 40 per cent in the all-white buildings. In Integrated II, the proportions are 48 per cent and 37 per cent respectively. Both these differences, however, are too small to be statistically significant.

It is interesting to note that at most 12 per cent in any proximity group in any of the four projects report management as disapproving of friendly Negro-white interaction. Evidently few residents in any of the projects find it conceivable that management should wish for anything but racial amity in a project.

Summary

In this chapter we have shown that in the four projects white house-wives living near Negro tenants are more likely to have intimate inter-racial contacts than are white housewives who live farther away. This relationship was found to hold even between the "finer" degrees of proximity.

Further data threw light on the conditions associated with close proximity which seemed to account for the development of interracial contacts. Thus, while all of the white women, regardless of where they lived in the project, were about equally likely to encounter Negro resi-dents by chance at the bus stop or at the project office, those living near Negroes were considerably more likely to encounter Negroes at the clothesline, in the parking areas (which are near the buildings), just outside the building, etc. Encounters in these latter places may be expected to occur with considerable frequency and to be of relatively prolonged duration. Bus stop, project office, and similar contacts are, as a rule, momentary and not so frequent.

Proximity of residence also makes feasible certain types of more inti-mate interracial contacts—borrowing and lending, helping out, baby-sitting, etc.—that lighten the burdens and problems of homemaking for the white women (as well, of course, as for the Negro). It seems reasonable to assume that the greater opportunities for these more inti-mate encounters for the white women living near Negroes laid the groundwork, in turn, for still further contacts of increasing social intimacy.

Our analysis suggests that the contacts which do occur are equal-status in character. They seem to have many of the characteristics of contacts between members of the same race: they are likely to involve children, interchange of services, and topics of conversation at all levels of intimacy. Many of the Negro-white contacts are reported as essen-tially neutral, neither pleasant nor unpleasant. It may be assumed that the contacts which fall into this category are primarily the more super-ficial ones. Among contacts where feeling tone is reported, the majority are pleasant, but, as would be expected in *any* interpersonal situation, some are unpleasant. White residents who live near Negroes are more likely than those living farther away to report contacts accompanied by some affect—and, in particular, to report pleasant experiences.

A second major finding was that white women living near Negroes were more likely than those living further away to perceive the opinions of other white women in the project as favorable to interracial contact. Our data suggest that the permissibility of friendly association with

Negroes is deduced in part from the actual observation by white residents of the characteristic level of interaction between other white residents and Negro residents. The very forces which make it likely that white women living in the same building or the same court with Negroes will have more than superficial contacts with them also make it likely that these same women will observe Negro-white interaction going on about them. Conversely when residents in a project are relatively distant from Negroes, the conditions which make contact unlikely also make it unlikely that other whites will be seen in interaction with Negroes.

The next chapter will reveal whether differences in proximity to Negroes, which gave rise to substantial differences in contact as well as to differences in perception of the social acceptability of such contact, were also accompanied by differences in ethnic attitude.

CHAPTER IV

Ethnic Attitude and Proximity

It was suggested in Chapter I that prejudice toward an ethnic minority arises relatively rarely from "bad" contacts with members of that minority but rather from the individual's exposure to society's prevailing attitudes toward the minority group in question. Ordinarily, an individual is continuously exposed to the same prejudiced environment from which he first absorbed his attitudes. Separation between the races appears to such an individual to be proper because it is supported at every turn by the practices and mores of society. It is a common tendency to believe that what is customary is right; to the prejudiced person it may appear that there would be no separation if there were not some good reason for it. Moreover, continued isolation from the ethnic minority helps maintain the beliefs and feelings about the minority group by removing the possibility of observing contrary evidence; whatever the individual has been led to believe about the minority in the course of growing up goes largely unchecked by direct evidence of his own senses.

One may argue that many people have contacts with Negroes in the course of everyday living. However, these contacts are generally of a very limited sort and are interpreted in particular ways. Thus, a Negro may be perceived as having personal characteristics contrary to stereotype, but these may be overlooked if the Negro occupies a subservient status. For example, a Negro domestic worker may be quite clearly industrious, pleasant, and polite, but she remains nevertheless a "menial" cleaning woman. Or, a Negro may be perceived as having not only characteristics but a status that is contrary to stereotypes, but such a Negro may then be said to be an exception, as in the case of the Negro professional person. Finally, the fact that discrimination against Negroes has placed them at a serious economic and cultural disadvantage increases the likelihood that a Negro whom the white person encounters may actually have characteristics interpretable as consistent with prevailing stereotypes.

Contacts of the sort reported in the previous chapter, however, in which Negroes and whites meet on equal terms and engage in more than superficial or stereotyped relationships, may counteract many of the factors which ordinarily operate to support prejudice.

In the first place, nearness of one's living quarters to those of Negroes may destroy the impression that separation is thought by society to be proper. With Negroes in the project, it may become apparent to many white residents that the governmental agency in charge considers "nearness" between the races appropriate. The contacts which occur among white and Negro residents who live close to one another operate, as we have seen, to foster the interpretation that such contacts are socially accepted. It is reasonable to suppose that what the white person believes should be done (i.e., his *policy orientation*) with respect to Negro-white relations may be affected by such circumstances.

Secondly, because the Negroes and whites in the project are of equal status (in the many ways predetermined by rental policies of the housing projects), the contacts that do take place are likely to destroy the foundation for many of the prejudiced *beliefs* held by the white tenant. Meeting Negro women who are like the white woman herself in many ways, including the roles they play in their families and in the project, very likely forces her to re-examine beliefs that Negroes are in some way "different" or inferior.

Thirdly, if the experiences which the white housewife has with Negroes in the project are essentially pleasant, or at least not unpleasant, it may be expected that her *feelings* toward Negroes will be affected.

The purpose of the present chapter is to consider the relation between proximity and ethnic attitudes in the four housing projects.* There is reason to believe that the various components of ethnic attitude—belief, feeling, and policy orientation—may not be affected alike by proximity. Attitudes may be thought of as extending along a dimension of specificity-generality. We shall consider as *specific* attitudes those having to do with the Negroes in the project or with situations of the particular type in which these Negroes have been encountered (i.e., public housing projects). We shall consider as *generalized* attitudes those having to do with Negroes in general, not only those living in the project, and with other nonwhite minority groups. In connection with the white residents' *specific* attitudes, we shall discuss separately the three components of belief, feeling, and policy orientation. As an adjunct to these data, a summary will follow of the findings concerning

---

*The relation between *contact* (as distinct from proximity) and attitude will be discussed in Chapter VII.

the attitudes of Negroes toward whites in the project. The discussion of the white residents' *generalized* attitudes will be brief and will not consider the three major components of attitude separately. .

Specific Attitudes

It was shown in the preceding chapter that white residents living near Negroes were more likely than those living farther away to engage in relatively intimate contacts with Negroes, to find these contacts pleasant, and to perceive a social climate approving of such contacts. It was hypothesized, therefore, that those living near Negroes would be more likely than those living farther away to be *favorable* in all aspects of attitude toward Negroes in the project and toward the idea of interracial public housing.

BELIEFS ABOUT NEGROES IN THE PROJECT

The white respondents were asked, as a measure of their belief in the similarity of Negroes and whites in the project, to compare white and Negro tenants on seven different characteristics. The questions were asked as follows: (1) "From what you've seen, who are the cleaner, the colored or the white or are they both about the same?" (2) ". . . whose children are better mannered?" (3) ". . . who helps more to keep the project in good condition?" (4) ". . . who are the more intelligent?" (5) "... who are the more ambitious?" (6) "... who in this project can be trusted more?" and (7) ". . . who are the more aggressive?" In all four of the projects on some items and in three out of four projects on other items, a smaller proportion of white respondents living near Negroes than of those living farther away indicated their belief in white superiority. For example, the distribution of responses on the first item, "cleanliness," among the housewives of Integrated I was as follows: among "nears," 14 per cent said whites

Table 13. Relation between Proximity and Degree of Belief in the Equality of Negroes and Whites in the Project

Number of Characteristics in Which Races Are Believed Equal	Integrated I		Building-Segregated I		Integrated II		Building-Segregated II	
	Near (73)	Far (107)	Near (77)	Far (95)	Near (113)	Far (145)	Near (58)	Far (138)
All 4	55%	28%	43%	26%	29%	22%	17%	20%
2 or 3	32	40	47	34	50	39	65	52
Only 1 or none ...	13	32	10	40	21	39	18	28
χ^2	14.7		19.2		8.9		3.6	
d.f.	2		2		2		2	
p	<.01		<.01		<.05		>.10	

were cleaner, 7 per cent said "colored," 76 per cent said "both the same," and 3 per cent said "don't know." The parallel figures for the "fars" were 27, 2, 66, and 5 per cent respectively.

Four of the items (1, 2, 3, and 4) formed a satisfactory unidimensional scale.* The findings for this scale are given in Table 13. Regular relationships were found in all the projects between proximity and belief in the equality of Negroes and whites in the project. In every project, there were considerably fewer among the white respondents living near Negroes than among those living farther away who considered Negro tenants equal to the white tenants on only a single characteristic or on no characteristic at all. At the other end of the scale, in the two moderate-rental projects (Integrated I and Building-Segregated I), substantially more "nears" than "fars" considered the two races equal in *all four* characteristics. In the two low-rental projects (Integrated II and Building-Segregated II) the differences disappear with regard to belief in similarity on all four characteristics but are maintained when three or fewer characteristics are considered. By and large, however, nearness to Negroes is associated with a greater likelihood of the white respondent's seeing *more* characteristics in which the races are similar.

The reason for this difference between "nears" and "fars" in beliefs about the characteristics of Negroes in the project lies probably in the fact that housewives living closer to Negroes have more opportunities to observe them. These daily observations, under circumstances of living in a relatively small community and associating with Negroes who have economic and social backgrounds similar to their own, increase the white respondents' awareness of the similarities between themselves and the members of the other race in numerous specific characteristics.

FEELINGS ABOUT NEGROES IN THE PROJECT

The second component of *specific* attitudes which was investigated concerned the feelings of the white respondents about the Negroes in the project. Although *beliefs* and *feelings* about a group are not necessarily perfectly related, in general it may be expected that those who hold favorable beliefs about the Negroes in the project will also be inclined to have positive feelings toward them.

* In constructing the scale—which was the unidimensional Guttman-type—the answer categories for each item were dichotomized: thus the responses "Negroes are better" and "Both the same" were combined as the responses favorable to Negroes for each of the four items. Choice of the favorable response was most frequent for items 2, 3, and 4, in that order. The coefficient of reproducibility for the scale was 91.5 per cent. The method used to test the scale was developed by Robert N. Ford and was described in "A Rapid Scoring Procedure for Scaling Attitude Questions," *Public Opinion Quarterly,* 1950, 14:507–532 (10).

Several questions were asked of the white respondents which made it possible to assess their feelings toward Negroes in the project in terms of the "esteem" in which they held the members of the other race.* Since the respondents answered this battery of questions in their own words and were encouraged to elaborate their answers, a comprehensive measure was obtained of the breadth and depth of their feelings toward Negroes in the project.

The following response by a white housewife living in a mixed court in Building-Segregated I is an example of an expression of positive feelings ("high esteem") for the Negroes in the project: "They are just like the white people as far as I am concerned. To me, one is the same as the other. If I invite neighbors in, I always invite the colored just as well—for TV, etc. They are always dressed neat; as clean as the white; polite, as far as I can see—very, very polite. . . . Their home is here as well as ours. They are friendly. . . . What more can you ask? I like the idea of mixing races because it helps promote good racial feeling. Why should there be all this talk about differences, or what you like or not? They seem to me the same in every way as the whites."

An example of the other extreme of feeling toward Negroes ("low esteem") is the response of a white respondent in a mostly all-white area in Building-Segregated II: "[The Negroes in this project are] like all colored people. They feel as if they own the world. They push themselves. They think they're a little better than most people. I hear that some of them in this project are very nice . . . but I wouldn't like them living in the next row. . . . They're in their element I guess when they live among white people. When they're in the South they can't do much but when they get up North and they find they can do a lot more things, they seem to take advantage of it. I suppose it's only human nature but I think they should be kept in their place. . . . I don't have any contact with them myself. I don't approve of their associating as close as they do in school . . ."

The expected difference between proximity groups in their relative "esteem" for Negroes was found consistently in each of the four projects, as can be seen in Table 14. In Integrated II, for example, 46 per cent of the white respondents living in mixed buildings expressed high "esteem" for Negroes in the project, compared to 31 per cent of the white respondents living in all-white buildings. In the other three projects as well, white tenants living near Negroes were more likely than those living farther away to express feelings indicating high

* The basic question used for classifying respondents regarding the "esteem" they felt for Negroes in the project was: "What about the colored people in this project, what are they like?" Answers to other questions about interracial aspects of project life were also consulted in making the classification.

Table 14. Relation between Proximity and Degree of "Esteem" for Negroes in the Project

Degree of Esteem	Integrated I		Building-Segregated I		Integrated II		Building-Segregated II	
	Near (73)	Far (107)	Near (77)	Far (95)	Near (113)	Far (145)	Near (58)	Far (138)
High	65%	43%	83%	42%	46%	31%	61%	50%
Mixed high and low	16	25	12	14	33	24	29	25
Low	18	32	4	35	21	39	7	23
Not classifiable	1	...	1	9	...	6	3	2
χ^2	8.9		33.5		9.8		6.7	
d.f.	2		2		2		2	
p	<.05		<.01		<.01		<.05	

"esteem" for the Negroes in their project. At the other end of the scale, in every project more "fars" than "nears" expressed feelings of *low* "esteem" for the Negroes in the project.

High esteem for the Negroes in the project—enjoying their friendship, appreciating their helpfulness, having good will toward them as people—does not necessarily mean wholehearted approval of *living* with Negroes. It is conceivable that a white resident's personal appraisal of Negroes is favorable, and yet this favorable appraisal may be accompanied by some discomfort stemming from the unaccustomed closeness of the races. For many residents even close personal experiences with Negroes may not be sufficient to offset the known and suspected counterpressures from the world outside the project.

The white respondents were asked, "How do you feel about living in a project like this where there are Negro and white families?" Although the wording of the question was the same in all projects, the answers, of course, have different referents depending on whether the respondent lived in an integrated or a building-segregated project.* The white respondents were also asked what things they liked and what things they did not like about the project. Each respondent's answers to the three questions were classified, first, according to approval or disapproval of living in a Negro-white project, and second, according to the positive and negative aspects mentioned about living in such a project. The respondents answered these questions in their own words and were urged to discuss them as fully as possible.

As shown by Table 15, there was a tendency in all four projects for proximity to be related to feelings about living in a mixed project. White respondents who lived relatively near Negroes were more likely

---

* The influence of *project type* on the responses will be discussed in Chapter VIII; here we shall consider only differences between proximity groups within each project.

Table 15. Relation between Proximity and Feelings about Living in a
Negro-White Project

Feeling	Integrated I		Building-Segregated I		Integrated II		Building-Segregated II	
	Near (73)	Far (107)	Near (77)	Far (95)	Near (113)	Far (145)	Near (58)	Far (138)
Approval	37%	20%	44%	34%	23%	18%	22%	25%
Mixed	27	28	42	25	15	15	43	28
Disapproval	36	50	13	33	60	65	33	42
Not classifiable ..	...	2	1	8	2	2	2	5
χ^2	7.2		9.0		1.1		2.7	
d.f.	2		2		2		2	
p	<.05		<.05		>.10		>.10	

to express some approval and less likely to express clear disapproval of interracial living than were those who lived farther away. The following comment by a white respondent illustrates approval of living in a biracial project: "It's a good and democratic way to live. In putting two races together, it helps understanding of the problems of both sides." Disapproval of the Negro-white character of the project was indicated by a white respondent in this way: "Don't like it at all. I suppose I'm bigoted, but they are forcing the issue down our throats." The differences between proximity groups were substantial in Integrated I and Building-Segregated I, less substantial in Integrated II and Building-Segregated II. For example, in Integrated I, 50 per cent of the white respondents who lived in all-white buildings expressed clear disapproval of living in a biracial project, as compared with 36 per cent of those living in mixed buildings. In Building-Segregated II, 42 per cent of the white respondents living in buildings *not* adjacent to a Negro building, as compared with 33 per cent of those who lived in buildings next to a Negro building, expressed clear disapproval of the biracial character of their project.

In other words, proximity is related not only to beliefs about and "esteem" for Negroes in the project, but also to the white respondent's feeling about living in an interracial project. However, fewer in each proximity group in a project like the biracial character of the project than have esteem for the Negroes there, thus bearing out the supposition that there are factors which impede acceptance of the idea of living with Negroes even when the specific Negroes are liked and respected. For example, among the white respondents who lived in mixed Negro-white buildings in Integrated I, 65 per cent expressed high esteem for the Negroes in the project, but only 37 per cent expressed unqualified approval of living in an interracial project. Among those

living in all-white buildings, 43 per cent expressed high esteem for the
Negroes in the project; only 20 per cent expressed unqualified approval
of interracial living.

In the *reasons* given for liking the interracial aspects of their respective projects we again encounter illuminating differences between
proximity groups. In every project, more "nears" than "fars" made
some positive comment about interracial living; as shown in Table 16,
the differences in proportions between proximity groups ranged from
11 per cent to 29 per cent. For instance, in Integrated I, 75 per cent
of those who lived in mixed buildings made *some* positive comment
about living in a project where there were Negroes, as compared to 46
per cent of those who lived in all-white buildings.*

Table 16 also gives the three positive characteristics of biracial projects that were mentioned most frequently by the white respondents.
The first has to do with pleasant traits and actions of Negro tenants
in the project. Among comments of this sort were: "They [the Negroes]
all seem pretty nice; seem clean; children better mannered than white,"
and "An older teen-age colored girl looks after my children. . . . Feel
that I can depend on that one person." As might be expected from our
knowledge of the relationship between proximity and "esteem," responses of this sort were given more frequently by white respondents
living near Negroes than by those living farther away. This is the case
in all four projects; our finding is that *at least* 12 per cent more of those
who live near Negroes than of those who live farther away give pleasant
traits or actions of Negroes as a basis for liking the biracial character of
their project.

Aside from the characteristics of the Negroes themselves as a basis
for liking the biracial character of the project, some white respondents
gave reasons that reflect respect for minority rights. For example, one
white respondent said, "I think it's more the American way—color or
race shouldn't make any difference," and other white respondents commented, "They [Negroes] have their rights," "They have to live as well
as we do," and "They are human the same as we are." In Integrated I,
40 per cent of the white respondents in mixed buildings mentioned
ideological factors of this kind, compared to 24 per cent of those in all-
white buildings. In the other three projects there was little difference
between the proximity groups in this respect; from one-fifth to one-
third of the white respondents in these projects, regardless of their
proximity to Negroes, mentioned ideological factors as a positive aspect
of living in a Negro-white project.

* Even some respondents who indicated clear disapproval of living in a biracial project
mentioned *some* positive aspects.

Table 16. Differences between Proximity Groups in Percentage Making Comments of a Positive Kind about Living in a Negro-White Project

Type of Positive Comment	Integrated I		Building-Segregated I		Integrated II		Building-Segregated II	
	Near (73)	Far (107)	Near (77)	Far (95)	Near (113)	Far (145)	Near (58)	Far (188)
Mention of any positive aspects of interracial living	75%	46%*	77%	53%*	51%	39%	71%	60%
Specific mention of:								
Pleasant traits and actions of Negroes	38	22*	38	14*	32	16*	34	22
Ideological factors	40	24*	31	37	23	22	36	37
Helping children avoid prejudice	22	7*	35	14*	4	3	16	12

* Differences are significant at least at the .05 level of confidence as calculated by the t test for significance of differences between percentages.

Finally, some white respondents saw biracial living as a beneficial experience for children. As one respondent said, "Children can be brought up to consider all equal," and another commented, "It teaches your children to get along with all kinds." A white respondent who lived in a mixed court in Building-Segregated I said: "At least my daughter will not point them [Negroes] out on the bus. She knows what they are by growing up with them. She will learn to respect *them* as well as white people." Table 16 shows that in two projects there were substantial differences between proximity groups in the proportions of white respondents who felt that living in a Negro-white project helped children avoid prejudice. These projects were Integrated I and Building-Segregated I, where, it should be noted, the proportion of young (and, in the eyes of parents, still malleable) children is much higher than in the other two projects.

Related to this concern for the effects of biracial living on children is another aspect of attitude connected with acceptance of living in a mixed project. This has to do with how parents feel about the interaction of Negro and white children. It has been suggested in Chapter III that children play an important role in bringing about contact with members of the other race, and that proximity is an important factor in this connection; white respondents living near Negroes were more likely than those living farther away to report that their children went into Negro children's homes to play, and that Negro children came into their homes to play. It might be expected, therefore, that differences would occur between the proximity groups in the proportions expressing approval or disapproval of Negro and white children playing together. Table 17 shows small but consistent differences in this respect in three of the four projects: Integrated I and II, and Building-Segregated II.

Table 17. Differences between Proximity Groups in Attitude toward Letting Negro and White Children Play Together

Attitude	Integrated I		Building-Segregated I		Integrated II		Building-Segregated II	
	Near (73)	Far (107)	Near (77)	Far (95)	Near (113)	Far (145)	Near (58)	Far (138)
Approval	73%	62%	83%	82%	56%	49%	57%	48%
Don't care one way or the other..	4	4	7	4	3	4	5	3
Disapproval	22	34	9	13	41	46	38	47
No answer	1	...	1	1	...	1	...	2
χ^2	3.4		0.9		1.5		1.6	
d.f.	2		2		2		2	
p	>.10		>.10		>.10		>.10	

In this section, then, we have seen a considerable amount of consistent evidence (although the differences between proximity groups are not always statistically significant) to support the hypothesis that white respondents living near Negroes are more likely than those living farther away to hold Negroes in high esteem and to approve of the biracial character of their project.

POLICY ORIENTATION WITH RESPECT TO OCCUPANCY PATTERN

It seems likely that a white resident's own feeling of comfort or discomfort at living in a biracial project would be paralleled by her opinion as to the policy to be followed in placing Negroes and whites in other public housing projects. It must be remembered, however, that when respondents reported their feelings about their projects, those living in the integrated projects were expressing approval or disapproval of an integrated occupancy pattern, while respondents in the building-segregated projects were expressing approval or disapproval of a building-segregated pattern.

The third component of *specific* attitudes, *policy orientation* with respect to interracial living, was measured by asking respondents in the four projects to recommend the occupancy pattern which "the city should follow in new projects."* The alternatives offered were that Negroes and whites should "live anywhere in the project," "in separate buildings," or "in separate projects."

Only in the integrated projects were respondents living near Negroes more likely than those living farther away to recommend that Negroes and whites be permitted to live "anywhere in the project" (i.e., in mixed buildings). In Integrated I, 44 per cent of white housewives living in the same building with Negroes recommended that Negroes and whites be assigned to apartments *anywhere* in the project, regardless of race, compared to 28 per cent of respondents in the all-white buildings; in Integrated II, the proportions were 20 per cent and 10 per cent in the mixed and all-white buildings respectively. Conversely, more "fars" than "nears" in these two projects recommended completely separate projects for whites and Negroes. This difference in the proportions recommending complete segregation appeared also in Building-Segregated I, where 32 per cent of respondents in all-white courts, compared to 18 per cent of those in mixed courts, recommended separate projects.

In other words, in three of the four projects, white respondents living near Negroes were more likely than those living farther away to

---

* This is considered an aspect of *specific* rather than general attitude because it refers directly to a situation of a particular type in which the respondent was at the time; that is, she was living in a public housing project of a particular occupancy pattern, and within the project she had a particular degree of proximity to Negroes.

recommend some arrangement whereby Negroes and whites would live in the same project. However, the recommendations for occupancy pattern in future projects were so complexly related to the occupancy pattern of the respondent's present project, as well as to her own feeling about the biracial character of her project, that they will be discussed in greater detail in Chapters VIII and IX, where the projects of different occupancy pattern are compared.

Attitudes of Negroes toward Whites in the Project

Although this study focuses primarily on the effect upon whites of residential proximity to Negroes, it is desirable for several reasons to examine also the attitudes of Negroes toward whites in the project. It is reasonable to assume that the development of contacts between races in the direction of more frequent neighborly activities will in part be dependent on the points of view held by Negro residents toward such contact.

It will be recalled from Chapter III that almost all the Negro respondents reported some kind of contact with whites in the project, at least half in each project reporting some kind of neighborly association. As was the case with the white respondents, Negro residents were also asked to describe the emotional tone of these contacts. At least three-quarters of the Negro housewives in three of the projects and about half in Building-Segregated II reported the contacts as pleasant; some of these, of course, as did the whites, reported unpleasant experiences as well. Fewer than 10 per cent in each project reported exclusively unpleasant experiences.

The Negro housewives were asked, in addition, about their "good friends" in the project. About three-fifths of the Negro respondents in the two moderate-rent projects reported that there were white women in the project with whom they were good friends; about two-fifths in the two low-rent projects made similar reports.

As might be expected, even the more neighborly contacts were not always considered by the Negro housewives as constituting close friendships with white women in the project. In each project, the proportion of Negro respondents who considered a white woman in the project as a good friend was smaller than the proportion who reported neighborly contact with whites. Moreover, in three of the four projects, the Negro respondents were more likely to report having close Negro friends than close white friends in the project; only in Integrated I did the Negro respondents report having as many close white friends as close Negro friends. It would appear, then, that in spite of the much larger number of white than Negro women in each project (which would mean more opportunities for friendships with white women, other things being equal), and in spite of considerable contact with the white residents, many Negro housewives found it easier to make friends with Negroes than with whites. This is illustrated by the comment of one Negro respondent who said she wished there were more Negroes in the project "because it is easier to make friends with colored people. You can present yourself to a colored person to make friends."

When asked to describe what the white people in the project were like, a majority of the Negro respondents made statements which indicated high regard for the whites, similar to the expressions of high "esteem" for the Negroes in the project which were made by the white respondents. One Negro housewife in Integrated I expressed positive feelings for the whites in the project in this way: "They are friendly, cooperative, and are not prejudiced. They're swell. They help to keep the building clean. We use the same reel for washing and we get along fine taking turns in sharing it." There were exceptions, however. A few expressed negative feelings, as illustrated by the following comment of a Negro housewife in Building-Segregated II: "They [the whites in the project] are trash. They are very poor and dirty. They don't seem to be as clean and intelligent as the Negro tenants living here. Although a thorough investigation is supposed to be made of all tenants before moving in, I think the Negro families are a better type."

Negro housewives were asked, finally, the identical question asked of white housewives regarding their recommendations for the occupancy pattern of future housing projects in the city. In three of the projects more than 90 per cent of the Negro respondents recommended the completely integrated arrangement—i.e., that applicants be given apartments anywhere in the project regardless of race. Only in Building-Segregated II were the proportions different: about half of the 39 Negro housewives recommending some other pattern, with 15 of these 20 women recommending separate buildings and 5 recommending completely separate projects.

The import of this brief review of Negro attitudes is that only a few Negro residents were actually hostile toward white residents in the project. Most Negroes liked the white persons in the project and a large majority in each project reported pleasant, or at least not unpleasant, contact experiences. Many felt genuinely at home in the projects and only 9 out of 145 Negro housewives interviewed desired completely segregated projects for the future. Whether the favorable attitudes of many Negroes in the projects toward white residents reflect change in attitude since moving in is an important question, and although obviously warranting investigation, was not the focus of the present study.

How do white respondents perceive and interpret the attitudes of Negro residents? Sensitivity to the feelings and desires of an ethnic minority has been held to be an indicator of the attitudes which members of a majority group hold toward that minority. It may be expected that isolation of a white resident from Negroes in the project ordinarily does not permit the white resident access to valid information regarding the attitudes of Negro residents. Under such circumstances, attribution of particular attitudes to Negroes may largely reflect these white residents' *own* attitudes. On the other hand, living near Negroes may give white tenants access to information more representative of the Negroes' true feelings and desires.

To determine whether there were systematic proximity-related differences in the interpretation of the attitudes of Negroes in the project, white residents were asked, first, whether they felt that the Negroes in the project preferred some sort of integration to complete segregation, and second, whether they thought the attitude of the Negroes in the project toward the white tenants was predominantly favorable or unfavorable. It was found that in all four projects, proximity was related to perception of the Negroes' preference for project-type. In Building-Segregated I in particular (the differences between proximity groups being significant) and in the other three projects to a lesser extent (the differences not being significant), white respondents living relatively near Negroes were more likely than those living farther away to believe that Negroes preferred some form of nonsegregated Negro-white living arrangement. In only two of the projects, however, were white women living near Negroes more likely than those living farther away to report it was their impression that the Negroes in the project had favorable feelings toward the white tenants. These were Building-Segregated I, where the difference was statistically significant, and Integrated II, where it was not. The comments of a white respondent living in a mixed court in Building-Segregated I are representative of statements by white housewives who perceived that the Negroes there preferred some form of integration: it "makes them feel as if they were wanted and not lower than white people." This respondent also perceived the Negroes in the project as having favorable feelings toward the white tenants there: "They just take us as humans, I suppose. They're friendly with us; no bad feeling between us."

Generalized Attitudes

We have seen that proximity to Negroes is related to favorable attitudes of white respondents toward the Negroes in the project. The question which we now wish to consider is one of generalization: To what extent does the alteration of attitude toward one minority sub-group (Negroes in a project) affect attitudes toward the minority group as a whole, and to what extent does it affect attitudes toward other minority groups having similar social definitions? Actually, the data in the earlier part of this chapter on attitude toward Negroes in the project are in themselves evidence of some generalization. Many respondents know only one, or a very few, Negroes in the project, and yet make statements characterizing most or all of them.

Granting the possibility of generalization of favorable attitude to Negroes in the project with whom one is not acquainted, the question remains whether the central reorganization of attitude has been sufficiently pervasive to make untenable former unfavorable stereotypes and beliefs regarding all Negroes. In what follows we will be alert to two possibilities: first, that favorableness of attitude may spread to "strangers" of the other race along all dimensions, and second, that the greatest generalization may take place with regard to items most directly connected with the contact experience itself.

ATTITUDES TOWARD NEGROES IN GENERAL

As in our procedure in measuring specific attitudes, so in measuring attitudes toward Negroes in general, we were interested in three aspects: belief, feeling, and policy orientation. However, because less interview time was devoted to the investigation of generalized attitudes, it was not possible to probe each aspect in detail. Two measures of generalized attitudes toward Negroes were used. One consisted of a series of five items adapted from the Negro subscale of the California Ethnocentrism Scale*; included were items referring to beliefs about the characteristics of Negroes in general and items referring to policy orientation with regard to Negro-white contact and status relationships. The other measure consisted of a series of "social distance" items, which were considered indicative of feeling about associating with various minority groups in certain specified situations.

Ethnocentrism Scale. The five items from the Ethnocentrism Scale were shown and read to the respondents toward the end of the interview. They were all worded in such a way that *agreement* signified derogation of Negroes generally. The following are the five items:

1. It would be a mistake ever to have Negroes as foremen and leaders over whites.

2. There may be a few exceptions, but in general, Negroes are pretty much alike.

3. The people who raise all the talk about putting Negroes on the

---

* See Adorno, *et al.* (2).

same level with whites are mostly radical agitators trying to stir up conflicts.

4. Most Negroes would become overbearing and disagreeable if not kept in their place.

5. Negroes have their rights but it is best to keep them in their own districts and schools and to prevent too much contact with whites.

An examination of the proportions of "nears" and "fars" in each of the projects who responded in a *prejudiced* way to each of the items (i.e., who agreed with each item) showed that while there appear to be some trends in the expected direction (that is, "nears" showing less prejudice) in all of the projects, in only one, Integrated I, do these trends approach significance.

Table 18. Differences between Proximity Groups in Amount of Agreement with Prejudiced Statements about Negroes in General

Number of Items Agreed with*	Integrated I		Building-Segregated I		Integrated II		Building-Segregated II	
	Near (73)	Far (107)	Near (77)	Far (95)	Near (113)	Far (145)	Near (58)	Far (138)
At most 1	40%	25%	39%	31%	9%	6%	12%	14%
2 or 3	31	26	33	28	27	20	28	26
4 or 5	29	49	28	41	64	74	60	60
χ^2	7.6		3.0		3.5		0.1	
d.f.	2		2		2		2	
p	<.05		>.10		>.10		>.10	

*Agreement indicates a negative attitude toward Negroes.

The five items were found to form a satisfactory unidimensional scale.* Table 18 shows the proportions agreeing with various numbers of items on this scale of generalized attitude toward Negroes; agreement with, at most, only one item represents the *most* favorable attitude, agreement with four or five items the *least* favorable. When the items are treated like this, a relationship appears between proximity and favorableness of generalized attitude in three of the four projects. In Integrated I, for example, 49 per cent of the white respondents living in all-white buildings took the most prejudiced position (agreed with 4 or 5 items), as compared with 29 per cent of those living in mixed buildings. In Building-Segregated I, 41 per cent of those in all-white courts, as compared with 28 per cent of those in mixed courts,

*In constructing the scale, the answer categories for each item were dichotomized: thus the response "disagree" was the response favorable to Negroes for each of the five items. Choice of the favorable response was most frequent for item 3, and next most frequent for items 4, 1, 5, and 2, in that order. The coefficient of reproducibility for the scale was 90.4 per cent.

took the most prejudiced position. Building-Segregated II was the only project in which there appeared to be no relation between proximity and favorableness of attitude toward Negroes in general; it will be recalled that this was the project in which there was the smallest relationship between proximity, on the one hand, and beliefs and feelings about the *specific* Negroes in the project, on the other.

In three of the projects, then, proximity is related to favorableness of attitudes toward Negroes in general, as measured by these five items from the Ethnocentrism Scale, as well as to favorableness of attitudes toward the specific Negroes in the project. Thus it would appear that some generalization of the more favorable specific attitudes does occur. However, the generalization is by no means complete. Table 14 showed that from 31 per cent to 83 per cent of the respondents in the various proximity groups in the four projects hold Negroes in the project in high esteem, and yet at most 17 per cent in any proximity group in any of the four projects reject *all* the prejudiced items in the scale of generalized attitudes. Some of the possible reasons for this discrepancy between specific and generalized attitudes will be discussed in later chapters.

Social distance. The physical and social distance one wishes to maintain between oneself and members of another ethnic group has long been recognized as an indicator of attitude toward that minority. There is reason to suppose that this dimension of generalized attitude may be related to how well white residents actually have accommodated to the "social distance" between themselves and the Negroes in the project, that is, to their feeling about living in a biracial project.

Toward the end of the interview the white respondents were asked to choose from a printed list of names of ethnic minorities those which they would not like their mayor to come from, would not like as tenants in the same building, would not like as schoolmates for their children, etc. One of the groups in the list was "Negroes."

Table 19 shows the proportion of respondents in the two proximity groups in each of the four projects who rejected Negroes in various capacities. Only in one of the projects, Integrated I, does there appear, on all the items, a sizeable and consistent relation between proximity and willingness to accept Negroes in the specified capacity. In Building-Segregated I, sizeable differences occur between proximity groups on only one item: those who live in mixed courts are less inclined than those in all-white courts to reject Negroes as fellow workers. In Integrated II, there is also only one capacity in which respondents who live in mixed buildings are less likely than those in all-white buildings to reject Negroes: as tenants of the same building. In Building-Segregated

Table 19. Differences between Proximity Groups in Their Desire to Maintain Social Distance, as Measured by Their Rejection of Negroes in Various Capacities

Capacity in Which Rejected	Integrated I		Building-Segregated I		Integrated II		Building-Segregated II	
	Near (73)	Far (107)	Near (77)	Far (95)	Near (113)	Far (145)	Near (58)	Far (188)
As mayor	42%	63%*	48%	46%	64%	66%	67%	63%
As tenants of the same building	42	67*	60	63	67	79*	81	75
As schoolmates of children	34	50*	29	40	65	66	60	56
As fellow club members	47	67*	51	55	73	72	66	72
As fellow workers	33	50*	27	43*	61	61	57	57

*Differences are significant at least at the .05 level of confidence as calculated by the t test for significance of differences between percentages.

Table 20. Differences between Proximity Groups in the Number of Capacities in Which Negroes Were Rejected

Number of Capacities	Integrated I		Building-Segregated I		Integrated II		Building-Segregated II	
	Near (73)	Far (107)	Near (77)	Far (95)	Near (113)	Far (145)	Near (58)	Far (138)
At most 1	57%	32%	42%	42%	25%	22%	17%	22%
2 or 3	8	16	26	14	14	17	31	23
4 or 5	35	52	32	44	61	61	52	55
χ^2	10.9		4.1		0.6		1.7	
d.f.	2		2		2		2	
p	<.01		>.10		>.10		>.10	

II there is no substantial difference between proximity groups on any item.

An "index of social distance" was constructed which included all five items. Table 20 shows to what degree the "nears" and "fars" in each project rejected Negroes—ranging from those who rejected Negroes in none or only one of the indicated capacities (the most favorable position) to those who rejected them in four or five capacities. The data combined in this way show findings similar to those for the individual items. In only one project, Integrated I, is there a marked difference between proximity groups; for example, 57 per cent of respondents living in mixed buildings rejected Negroes in, at most, only one capacity, as compared with only 32 per cent of those in all-white buildings. In the two building-segregated projects there is only a slightly greater tendency for "nears" than for "fars" to reject Negroes in fewer capacities, and in Integrated II there are no differences between proximity groups in the number of capacities in which Negroes were rejected.

The items chosen to measure desired social distance represent hypothetical social situations, removed in various degrees from the kind of situation in which the white respondents are currently in contact with Negroes. Obviously the second item of Table 19 ("as tenants of the same building") is the one closest to the respondents' present experience; it is therefore of interest to consider this item in particular detail. Only in the integrated projects is there a substantial difference between proximity groups. In Integrated I, 67 per cent of those living in all-white buildings, as compared with 42 per cent of those in mixed buildings, name Negroes as a group they would not like to have living in the same building. In Integrated II the proportions are 79 per cent and 67 per cent in the all-white and mixed buildings, respectively. In both of the building-segregated projects, "nears" and "fars" are *equally* likely to react negatively to the idea of Negroes living in the same building with them. This is in keeping with the finding, reported earlier in this chapter, that only in the integrated projects were "nears" more likely than "fars" to recommend that Negroes and whites be permitted to live *anywhere* in future projects (i.e., to recommend mixed buildings). Here again it appears that occupancy pattern modifies the influence of proximity. The influence of occupancy pattern on desired social distance will be discussed in Chapter VIII.

ATTITUDES TOWARD OTHER MINORITIES

None of the projects in the present study included more than one per cent of nonwhite groups other than Negroes. It was thus possible, by assessing attitudes toward two other minorities, to arrive at an estimate of the influence of proximity to Negroes on general attitudes toward other minorities. The two groups chosen for analysis were Chinese and Puerto Ricans. Since the numbers of Chinese and Puerto Ricans in the projects were negligible, differences between proximity groups in expressed attitude toward them could not be attributed to contact with them, but rather must be considered in some way an extension of the generalization of attitude toward Negroes, the large nonwhite minority in the projects.

Chinese and Puerto Ricans were among the ethnic groups from which respondents were asked to choose those they would prefer *not* to have in the position of mayor or as co-tenants, fellow workers, etc. Table 21 shows the proportions of those living near Negroes and those living far from Negroes who reacted negatively to the idea of admitting these other nonwhite groups to equal status in various ways. In three of the projects there are no systematic or significant differences between proximity groups in their rejection of Chinese and Puerto Ricans. In only one project, Integrated I, are there systematic differences between those living in Negro-white buildings and those living in all-white buildings (and only one of these differences is statistically significant). In this particular project, from 12 to 14 per cent fewer of the "nears" than of the "fars" express a desire to exclude Chinese in all the capacities specified. The differences on *each* item between proportions of "nears" and "fars" who reject Puerto Ricans are in the same direction but are smaller. Furthermore, the differences between proximity groups in the proportions rejecting Chinese and Puerto Ricans in each of the capacities are smaller than the differences between proximity groups in the proportions rejecting Negroes in the same capacities.

Summary

The data presented in this chapter tend to support the hypothesis that white residents who live relatively near Negroes will be more

Table 21. Differences between Proximity Groups in the Degree to Which Chinese and Puerto Ricans Were Rejected in Various Capacities

Capacity in Which Rejected	Integrated I		Building-Segregated I		Integrated II		Building-Segregated II	
	Near (73)	Far (107)	Near (77)	Far (95)	Near (113)	Far (145)	Near (58)	Far (188)
As mayor								
Chinese	45%	58%	62%	53%	53%	49%	50%	41%
Puerto Ricans	40	49	52	42	35	38	29	22
As tenants of the same building								
Chinese	49	62	64	59	57	51	53	50
Puerto Ricans	40	47	53	48	42	41	36	28
As schoolmates of children								
Chinese	30	44*	31	41	40	38	33	30
Puerto Ricans	30	36	25	35	24	32	22	22
As fellow club members								
Chinese	44	56	52	53	44	42	33	45
Puerto Ricans	41	45	45	44	37	37	29	29
As fellow workers								
Chinese	32	44	30	43	42	39	31	36
Puerto Ricans	26	34	26	38	36	37	21	25

*Difference is significant at least at the .05 level of confidence as calculated by the t test for significance of differences between percentages.

likely than those who live farther away to accept the idea of Negroes
and whites living together, to have favorable beliefs about and feelings
toward Negroes in the project, and to have favorable attitudes toward
Negroes in general.

On all aspects of *specific* attitudes which were measured, there was
some tendency—though not always statistically significant—for more
white respondents living near Negroes than those living farther away
to express favorable attitudes. In all four projects, "nears" were more
likely than "fars" to consider Negroes in the project equal to the white
tenants on a number of characteristics, to hold the Negroes in the
project in high esteem, and to express *some approval* of the interracial
character of their project. In three of the four projects, "nears" were
more likely than "fars" to recommend for the future some occupancy
pattern other than completely separate projects for Negroes and whites.

One aspect of *generalized* attitudes—favorableness toward Negroes
in general, as measured by the California Ethnocentrism Scale—was
shown to have some relation to proximity. In one project, proximity
was definitely related to favorableness of attitudes toward Negroes in
general. In two other projects there was at least a tendency in that
direction. However, the more favorable *specific* attitudes of the "nears"
were by no means completely generalized. A greater proportion of
"nears," as well as of "fars," held Negroes in the project in high esteem
than rejected *all five* of the prejudiced items on the Ethnocentrism Scale.

The measurement of social distance with respect to Negroes, another
aspect of *generalized* attitudes, showed that in only one project were
there significant differences between proximity groups; in two others
there were slight differences in the expected direction; in the fourth
project no difference appeared. With respect to social distance toward
two other nonwhite minorities (Chinese and Puerto Ricans), differences
between proximity groups were with one exception not statistically
significant.

It appears, then, that proximity is related to favorableness of attitude toward the specific Negroes in the contact situation and to acceptance of the particular interracial experience. Moreover, the more favorable attitudes of the "nears" toward the specific Negroes are generalized to some extent, but by no means completely, to Negroes as a group.
There is a slight tendency, too, for the greater acceptance of the particular interracial experience on the part of the "nears" to be generalized to acceptance of Negroes in other social situations. Generalization
to other nonwhite minorities, however, appears to be the least likely,
at any rate under the circumstances obtaining in the projects of this
study.

CHAPTER V

Initial Comparability of
"Nears" and "Fars"

THROUGHOUT the preceding chapters we have made the assumption that "nears" and "fars" were initially comparable and that the observed differences in extent of contact, etc., could be attributed to the influence of proximity. The validity of this assumption is, of course, crucial to the interpretation of findings throughout the study. If more "nears" than "fars" held favorable attitudes toward Negroes and toward interracial association at the time they moved into the projects, current differences between them could not justifiably be interpreted as revealing the effects of living in greater or lesser proximity to Negroes in the project. In this chapter we shall present evidence for the assumption that in each project "nears" *as a group* and "fars" *as a group* were in fact similar in prior experience with, and attitude toward, Negroes at the time they moved into the projects.

There were, of course, *within* each proximity group indications of differences in initial attitudes among the white residents. These differences make it possible to assess the influence of initial attitude within each proximity group and to investigate the interaction of proximity and initial disposition in affecting ethnic attitudes. These points will be discussed in the following chapter.

What are the possible biasing factors that could increase the likelihood of initially less prejudiced individuals' living near Negroes? Such a situation could conceivably come about either through managerial policies or through self-selection on the part of the tenants. Since this was an ex post facto study, it was not possible to get definitive measures of the ethnic attitudes which our respondents had held at the time they moved into the projects. In the absence of such measures, information of three sorts was gathered to check on the possibility that "nears" and "fars" might have differed systematically in initial attitudes: (1) factors directly related to the project situation—rental policies, refusals of apartments by prospective residents, move-out rates, preference for project, etc.; (2) background characteristics or experiences known to be generally correlated with ethnic attitude—religion, education, political attitude, reported opinions of friends, etc.; and (3) respondents' own reports of prior attitude toward Negroes. In this section we shall present data from which the initial attitudes of "nears" and "fars" may be deduced and we shall consider the possibility that there were situational factors other than proximity to Negroes which affected the two groups differently.*

Factors Directly Related to the Project Situation
MANAGERIAL POLICIES

It is conceivable that rental policy in some way led to biased selection of tenants in the different proximity groups. It may be, for example, that managers, concerned with keeping peace within their projects, tend systematically to avoid placing the more outspokenly prejudiced white applicants in apartments near Negroes and, instead, offer such applicants available apartments in locations relatively distant from those occupied by Negroes.

In all four of the projects the stated rental policies were such as to make it unlikely that ethnic attitudes were taken into account in the assignment of apartments. In the very earliest stages of the study, we conducted interviews with the local managers and other project and housing authority personnel, and at that time we asked a great many questions about the application of the rental policies. In every case, it appeared unlikely that there had been any systematic assignment of less prejudiced persons to apartments relatively near Negroes or of more prejudiced persons to apartments farther away. In all four cities

* Even if the two groups were comparable at the time of moving in, it is conceivable that there may have been some systematic factors within the project situation (such as special facilities available to one group and not the other) which operated differently for the two groups. If white residents living near Negroes received better treatment from management than did the white residents living farther away, this fact might have contributed to the "near"-"far" differences we have observed. Such possible differential treatment, whether accidental or planned, represents situational factors that, while not throwing direct light on the problem of initial comparability, might conceivably have differentially promoted or hindered the development of favorable attitudes, etc., in the two comparison groups in each project. However, from interviews with managers, and from the authors' inspection tours in all four of the projects, it seemed clear that in such items as care of buildings, walks, and grounds, and promptness in making repairs, white tenants received equal service whether they lived near to or far from Negroes. Furthermore, in each of the four projects, all white tenants, regardless of distance from the Negroes in the project, have about equal facilities for hanging clothes and for parking cars, are at about the same distance from markets and transportation stops, etc.

assignments were made from a central tenant-selection office without knowledge of where, within the project, the particular apartment was located in relation to a Negro-occupied apartment.

SELF-SELECTION

Regardless of managerial policy, a process of self-selection might go on among the tenants. The more prejudiced white families might refuse apartments close to Negroes, or finding themselves in such apartments, might move out. We therefore asked the project managers about refusal rates and examined the records of move-outs.

It appeared unlikely that there was any systematic tendency for apartments near Negroes to be refused. In each of the four projects the management reported that there were occasional refusals by eligible applicants who had, since the date of application, found a suitable apartment or had perhaps moved to another city or part of the city or required more or fewer rooms because of increases or diminutions in family size. But such refusals generally took place immediately upon notification, without the applicant's even inspecting the apartment. According to the reports of the project managers, it very rarely happened that an apartment was turned down for *any* reason once the applicant had maintained his interest sufficiently to visit the designated apartment. In Integrated II, for example, the assistant manager informed us that over a period of about three years, during which he had rented apartments to 600 tenants, only 6 applicants rejected apartments after they had seen them. The information obtained from the managers of the other three projects also supports the conclusion that self-selection on the basis of ethnic attitude, at the time of moving in, was unlikely.

There is, furthermore, still another condition which may be assumed to operate against the likelihood of preselection on the basis of ethnic attitude. This is the fact that each of the projects of our study happened to have certain intrinsic advantages which would tend to lead applicants to accept apartments in these particular projects even if they anticipated some discomfort from living near Negroes. Three of the projects offered the best public housing facilities available in the area. Integrated I and Building-Segregated I were the *newest* public housing projects in their respective cities at the time most of our respondents moved in. Integrated II was the only *permanent* low-rental public housing development in its part of the city; the temporary developments close by were far less comfortable and attractive. Thus it seems likely that more prejudiced applicants might be inclined to accept an apartment *anywhere* in one of these three projects, even if it meant living relatively near a Negro family, rather than live in a less satisfactory development. Building-Segregated II did not have this characteristic of being superior to all other public housing developments in the vicinity. However, it had a *smaller proportion of Negroes* than any of the other projects in the city, all but one of which had the identical building-segregated occupancy pattern. A prejudiced person might conceivably accept an apartment in this project, even if it were relatively close to Negroes, rather than in another project which had a larger Negro population.

Our interpretation is that there was little likelihood of bias, either through management policy or self-selection, in the assignment of apartments. Nevertheless, it is still possible that there may have been systematic differences between the white residents who moved out of the projects and those who stayed. It may be that those who lived relatively near Negroes were more likely to move out than those who lived farther away, and it is possible that those who did move out were the more prejudiced white residents. Thus differential move-out rates between "nears" and "fars" might indicate a systematic process of self-selection leading to a greater concentration of less prejudiced individuals among the "nears."

A simple measure of this possibility is the relative white move-out rate from apartments in the two proximity groups. White move-out rates in the four projects ranged from 15 per cent to 25 per cent a year. An analysis of the move-out records was made in each of the four projects. In the two segregated projects a comparison was made of move-outs from buildings adjacent to and not adjacent to a Negro building; the "near" and "far" buildings were always the same. In the two integrated projects, a white move-out was considered a "near" if at the time of the move-out there was a Negro family living in the building, a "far" if at the time of the move-out the building was occupied entirely by white families.

The findings showed similar move-out rates for the two proximity groups in each of the projects; such differences as existed could easily have occurred by chance. In Integrated II, for example, where the highest total move-out rate for all the projects occurred, the difference in the rate between white residents living in mixed buildings and those living in all-white buildings was only 3 per cent. The figures in the other projects similarly argue against differential move-out rates.

In addition to these items of objective evidence, questions were asked in the interview about the respondent's preference for a given project at the time of application and about prior knowledge of the biracial character of the project. It was reasoned that if there had been no bias either in original assignment and acceptance of apartments or in differential move-out rates, the two proximity groups should be similar in the proportions who had expressed a preference for their present project and who knew in advance that there would be Negroes in the project. Had there been a greater proportion of originally unprejudiced persons among the "nears," it might be expected that there would be a greater proportion among the "nears" than among the "fars" who had preferred the project of present occupancy and who had known of the presence of Negroes in the project before moving in.

In every project strikingly similar proportions of "nears" and "fars" reported that at the time of application they preferred the project they were in to some other project in the city. The largest difference—which fell considerably short of statistical significance—was found in Building-Segregated I, where, of those who had a preference at the time of application, 90 per cent now living in the mixed courts and 83 per cent now living in all-white courts preferred this project to others in the city.

Nor was there any marked difference between "nears" and "fars" in any project in the proportions who reported knowing, at the time they were offered an apartment, that there were Negroes in the project. The largest difference was found in Integrated I, where 52 per cent of the white respondents living in mixed buildings reported knowing of the biracial character of the project, compared to 59 per cent of those in all-white buildings. This difference, too, falls far short of statistical significance.

In summary, all sources of information directly related to the project situation—managerial policies, reports of refusals of apartments, move-out rates, original preference for project, and prior knowledge of the biracial character of the project—show no differences between "nears" and "fars." The evidence up to this point, then, supports the hypothesis that there was no systematic selection and that "nears" and "fars" were originally comparable.

Other Correlates of Initial Attitude

So far we have been drawing inferences from data directly related to the project situation which would seem logically to give some indication of the initial comparability of "nears" and "fars." It is possible to attempt to estimate initial attitudes in another way, namely, on the basis of personal characteristics and experiences which have been demonstrated in a number of studies to be correlated with ethnic attitude. In the absence of direct measures of attitude at the time the respondents moved in, it is not possible, of course, to establish the absolute level of initial attitude; however, it is possible from these indirect indicators to determine whether respondents were more or less favorably disposed toward Negroes at the time of moving in.

PERSONAL BACKGROUND

A number of studies have suggested that attributes such as religion, education, and political-economic attitudes are correlated with ethnic attitudes. These were the kinds of personal characteristics about which we obtained information from the white respondents; we shall now utilize the data as further indicators of the extent of initial comparability between proximity groups within each of the projects.

While there are some differences *between* projects in *religious distribution, within* each project the proportions of Protestants, Catholics, and Jews are almost identical in the two proximity groups. The figures are shown in the first item of Table 22. To the extent that religion may be taken as a partial indicator of probable initial attitude, these data support the hypothesis that "nears" and "fars" were similar in ethnic attitudes at the time of moving into the projects.

There is greater variation between proximity groups with respect to *education.* In both of the building-segregated projects there are prox-

Table 22. Distribution within the Various Proximity Groups of Personal Characteristics Believed to Be Correlated with Initial Attitude

Personal Characteristic	Integrated I		Building-Segregated I		Integrated II		Building-Segregated II	
	Near (73)	Far (107)	Near (77)	Far (95)	Near (113)	Far (145)	Near (58)	Far (138)
Religion								
Protestant	23%	23%	35%	32%	27%	32%	40%	38%
Catholic	70	69	64	63	67	61	58	60
Jewish	4	7	...	3	4	3	2	1
Other, none, etc.	3	1	1	2	2	4	...	1
Education								
Eighth grade or less	10	9	12	5*	47	40	9	25*
Some high school	37	26	37	25	33	34	49	46
Completed high school	48	59	42	56	14	19	38	23
Some college or more	5	6	9	14	6	7	4	6
Political attitude								
Liberal	33	31	28	21	39	45	26	35
Middle of the road	39	34	46	40	30	33	29	28
Conservative ..	28	35	26	39	31	22	45	37

* Differences are significant at the .05 level of confidence by the χ^2 test.

imity-related differences greater than might be expected by chance; however, the differences are in opposite directions in the two projects. The figures are shown in the second item of Table 22. In Building-Segregated I, 70 per cent of those living in all-white courts have at least completed high school, as compared with 51 per cent of those in mixed courts—a difference of 19 per cent. In Building-Segregated II, on the other hand, those living farther from Negroes are likely to have had *less* education than those living near Negroes; 25 per cent of the "fars," as compared with 9 per cent of the "nears," have not gone beyond the eighth grade. Since most studies have shown that prejudice diminishes as education increases, it would appear that only in Building-Segregated II was there a possibility of bias in initial attitude which would affect the interpretation of our findings; that is, to the extent that initial attitude can be estimated from educational level, only in Building-Segregated II were "nears" more likely than "fars" to be favorably predisposed toward Negroes.

The third item of Table 22 shows scores on an index of political attitudes based on five items adapted from the California Scale of Political-Economic Conservatism. The items used tapped attitude toward labor unions, government ownership, the rights of radicals to become citizens, etc. Since the study by Adorno *et al.* (2) found a correlation of the order of 0.8 between prejudice and political-economic conservatism among several populations of working-class women (similar to our respondents), the scores on this index would seem to be a fair indicator of probable initial ethnic attitude. In every project there is a small difference between "nears" and "fars" in political-economic attitude. In the two low-rental projects (Integrated II and Building-Segregated II), there are somewhat *more* conservatives among the "nears" than among the "fars"; such differences might be expected to operate against a more favorable initial attitude among the "nears." In Integrated I and Building-Segregated I, however, there were somewhat *fewer* conservatives among the "nears" than among the "fars"; the trend in these two projects, then, suggests a possible slight bias in the direction of more favorable initial attitudes on the part of the "nears," though differences are not significant statistically.

ASSOCIATIONS AND EXPERIENCES

Certain past or continuing associations and experiences may be thought of as probably related to ethnic attitudes—either as reflecting such attitudes or as influencing them. One such experience is prior association with Negroes; another is the attitudes of relatives and friends toward association with Negroes.

It is pointed out in the review of literature (see Appendix) that a number of studies have found a correlation between prior equal-status contact with Negroes and present favorable attitude toward them. It seems reasonable to suppose that the correlation held also for our respondents at the time of moving into the project. We do not know to what extent the previous contact reflected already favorable attitudes or to what extent (in line with the hypotheses of the present study) it may have led to favorable attitudes. In any event, the extent of previous contact with Negroes, whatever the nature of its relationship to ethnic attitude, may be presumed to have a bearing on the initial comparability of "nears" and "fars" in the projects.

Respondents were asked whether, before moving into the project, they had had Negro friends or acquaintances, had worked with Negroes, and/or had lived near Negroes. Table 23 shows the proportions of "nears" and "fars" in each project who had had various amounts of contact with Negroes before moving into the project. As can be seen, there is relatively little difference between proximity groups in any project in the number of kinds of previous contacts reported. The largest difference—which is not statistically significant— is found in Building-Segregated I, where 41 per cent of the respondents in mixed courts, compared to 33 per cent in all-white courts, report two or more kinds of prior contact with Negroes.

Table 23. Distribution within the Various Proximity Groups of Whites Who Had Had Prior Contact with Negroes*

	Integrated I		Building-Segregated I		Integrated II		Building-Segregated II	
Prior Contact†	Near (73)	Far (107)	Near (77)	Far (95)	Near (113)	Far (145)	Near (58)	Far (138)
All 3 kinds	8%	6%	14%	7%	8%	4%	7%	9%
Any 2 kinds	23	21	27	26	15	21	28	23
Any 1 kind	32	31	33	35	34	33	31	30
None	37	42	26	32	43	42	34	38

*None of the comparisons was significant at the .05 level of confidence by the χ^2 test.

†Respondents were asked about three kinds of experience with Negroes prior to moving into the project: (a) whether they had Negro friends or acquaintances before the move, (b) whether they had worked with Negroes, and (c) whether they had lived near Negroes.

Of the items making up the index of prior contact, those concerning prior friendships with Negroes and prior residence near Negroes merit further consideration because of their close correspondence to the variables in the present study. Although there are substantial differences *between* projects in the proportion of white respondents who reported having Negro friends or acquaintances before they moved into the project, there is a striking similarity between "nears" and "fars" *within* each project in this respect. A typical instance is Integrated II, where 23 per cent of those who live in mixed buildings, and 24 per cent who live in all-white buildings, report such prior acquaintance.

In none of the projects is the difference between the proportions of "nears" and "fars" who report prior residence near Negroes greater than might easily have occurred by chance. Even though not statistically significant, there is, however, in Building-Segregated I the possibility of a slight initial bias that should be noted. In this particular project a somewhat *greater* proportion of "nears" than of "fars" report having lived in the same block with Negroes before moving into the project (22 per cent of "nears" and 12 per cent of "fars"). On the other hand, a somewhat *smaller* proportion of "nears" than of "fars" in Integrated II report having lived in the same block with Negroes before moving into the project, but again the differences are not statistically significant.

It has been demonstrated a number of times that there is a relation between one's own attitudes and those of friends and relatives. With respect to the idea of living in a biracial project, it may be supposed that the attitudes of the project residents had changed more than those of their friends and relatives outside the project. Thus, it may be supposed that an estimate of the attitude of these "outsiders" toward living in a biracial project would provide some indication of the attitudes held by our respondents before they moved into the projects. If there had been biased apartment assignment, it might be expected that a greater proportion of "nears" than of "fars" would report that their friends approve of their living in a project where there are Negroes.

The respondents' replies to a question asking how their friends and relatives felt about their living in a mixed project are shown in Table 24. It can be seen that there is no *significant* relation between proximity to Negroes within the project and the reported views of relatives and friends outside the project; such differences as do exist might easily have occurred by chance. To the extent that the reported attitudes of friends and relatives may be taken as a partial clue to the attitudes of the respondents at the time they moved into the projects, these findings are consistent with the hypothesis that there were no initial differences in attitudes between proximity groups within a project.

Each of the factors just considered taken separately is, of course, a fallible indicator of initial attitude. A somewhat better estimate of the original disposition of tenants in the different proximity groups within a project may be obtained by combining several of the factors into an

Table 24. Distribution within the Various Proximity Groups of Reported Reactions of Relatives and Friends outside the Project*

Reported Reaction	Integrated I		Building-Segregated I		Integrated II		Building-Segregated II	
	Near (73)	Far (107)	Near (77)	Far (95)	Near (113)	Far (145)	Near (58)	Far (138)
Most approve	35%	28%	36%	34%	21%	18%	39%	31%
A few approve ...	21	19	8	4	12	10	9	9
None approve ...	32	31	9	12	41	43	19	23
Don't care one way or the other..	10	19	44	47	21	19	24	25
Don't know, no relatives	2	3	3	3	5	10	9	12

* None of the comparisons was significant at the .05 level of confidence by the χ^2 test.

index of estimated initial attitude. Such an index was constructed on the basis of the following five items: religion, education, political-economic attitudes, previous contact with Negroes, and prior knowledge that there were Negroes in the project. These five items were chosen because preliminary analysis showed that individually they bore the closest relation to respondents' ethnic attitude, regardless of proximity. Each item was scored as indicating a probable pro-Negro position or a probable anti-Negro position, and respondents were classified as having the pro-Negro position on four or five, on two or three, and on one or no items.

Table 25 shows how "nears" and "fars" in each project compare on this index. In only one of the projects, Building-Segregated II, is there a very slight—and not statistically significant—trend toward a greater proportion of those living near Negroes than of those living farther away to have had relatively favorable attitudes toward Negroes at the time of moving in. On the other hand, in Integrated II, where the only statistically significant difference occurs, the difference between prox-

Table 25. Distribution of Tenants in the Various Proximity Groups on an Index of Estimated Initial Attitude toward Negroes

Number of Items Indicating Probable Pro-Negro Position	Integrated I		Building-Segregated I		Integrated II		Building-Segregated II	
	Near (73)	Far (107)	Near (77)	Far (95)	Near (113)	Far (145)	Near (58)	Far (138)
4 or 5	12%	20%	19%	18%	8%	5%*	10%	13%
2 or 3	59	55	57	64	51	68	77	67
0 or 1	29	25	24	18	41	27	13	20

* Difference is significant at the .05 level of confidence by the χ^2 test.

imity groups with respect to the index suggests that a greater proportion of "fars" than of "nears" had initially favorable attitudes. The index supports the supposition derived from examination of the individual items that "nears" did not hold more favorable initial attitudes toward Negroes than did "fars."

IMPRESSIONS OF NEGROES BEFORE MOVING INTO THE PROJECT

Up to this point we have been presenting objective data which are believed to offer clues to the probable ethnic attitudes of "nears" and "fars" at the time they moved into the projects. Another approach, of course, is to ask people for their recollection of their own attitudes. What a person recalls of a prior experience is admittedly open to error or distortion for a variety of reasons; despite the risk of some inaccuracy of report, we asked our respondents what they had thought colored people were like prior to moving into the project. The supposition was that if there had been systematic differences in attitude between "nears" and "fars" at the time of moving in, they would be reflected in greater than chance differences in recalled impressions of Negroes.

The findings given in Table 26 again support the hypothesis that "nears" and "fars" were comparable in initial attitude toward Negroes. In none of the four projects are the differences between proximity groups larger than could easily have occurred within the customary probability limits. For instance, in Integrated II, 25 per cent of those living in mixed buildings reported predominantly positive initial impressons, and 61 per cent predominantly negative; in the all-white buildings the analogous figures were 28 per cent and 56 per cent. In two of the projects, Integrated I and Building-Segregated II, the differ-

Table 26. Comparability of the Various Proximity Groups in Their Reported Impressions of Negroes before Moving into the Project *

Reported Impression	Integrated I		Building-Segregated I		Integrated II		Building-Segregated II	
	Near (73)	Far (107)	Near (77)	Far (95)	Near (113)	Far (145)	Near (58)	Far (138)
Predominantly positive	33%	23%	40%	36%	25%	28%	29%	38%
Both negative and positive, or indifferent	12	23	18	23	8	14	19	22
Predominantly negative	53	51	38	37	61	56	50	34
Don't know, not classifiable	2	3	4	4	6	2	2	6

* None of the comparisons was significant at the .05 level of confidence by the χ^2 test.

ences are somewhat more substantial, but even in these projects they are still too small to be statistically significant.

Summary

In attempting to determine whether "nears" and "fars" were similar in ethnic attitudes at the time of moving into the projects, various kinds of data were gathered which might give clues as to possible initial attitude. These data were of three kinds: factors within the project situation directly related to the possibility of biased apartment assignment or selection; factors known to be generally correlated with ethnic attitude, such as religion, education, political attitude, and attitude of friends toward interracial association; and respondents' own reports of their impressions of Negroes prior to moving in. On only one item—education—were there significant differences between "nears" and "fars" in any project; however, in the two projects where there were significant differences between proximity groups in this respect, the differences were in opposite directions. Taken both as individual items and as a whole, the data strongly support the hypothesis that "nears" and "fars" within any given project were similar in ethnic attitude at

Table 27. Summary Chart Comparing "Nears" and "Fars" on Various Items Considered Indicators of Probable Initial Attitude toward Negroes*

Item	Building-Integrated I	Segregated I	Building-Integrated II	Segregated II
Management rental policies	=	=	=	=
Refusal of apartments	=	=	=	=
Move-out rates	=	=	=	=
Original preference for project ...	=	>	=	>
Knowledge of presence of Negroes	<	<	>	=
Religion	=	=	<	=
Education	<	<<	<	>>
Political attitude	>	>	<	<
Prior contact with Negroes, Index	>	>	=	=
Prior friendship with Negroes ...	=	=	=	=
Prior residence near Negroes	=	>	<	=
Attitudes of friends	>	=	=	>
Index of estimated initial attitude	=	=	<<	>
Own report of prior impressions..	>	=	=	<

* Key: = indicates little or no difference in distribution between "nears" and "fars"
   > indicates *more* (but not significantly) "nears" than "fars" in position believed to indicate probable favorable predisposition toward Negroes
  >> indicates *significantly more* "nears" than "fars" in position believed to indicate probable favorable predisposition toward Negroes
   < indicates *fewer* (but not significantly) "nears" than "fars" in position believed to indicate probable favorable predisposition toward Negroes
  << indicates *significantly fewer* "nears" than "fars" in position believed to indicate probable favorable predisposition toward Negroes.

the time of moving into the project, or in the few instances in which they differed, the data were likely to indicate that "fars" were somewhat more favorably disposed.

The data from which inferences about initial attitude were drawn have been presented in considerable detail because the question of initial comparability of proximity groups is central to the interpretation of our findings. A summary of the factors considered is given in chart form in Table 27 in order to make available at a glance all the data bearing on probable initial attitude. From this chart it can easily be seen that in every project, on just over half of the items there was little or no difference in distribution between "nears" and "fars"; that on all but three of the others such differences as did appear were not statistically significant; and that where differences did occur, they were inconsistent from item to item rather than following a systematic trend.

The logical conclusion of the preceding discussion is that the differences between proximity groups reported in earlier chapters reflect the differential effects of living relatively close to or far from Negroes in the project. If similar distributions of original attitudes occurred among the white residents in the proximity groups being compared, then the more favorable attitudes now current among the white housewives living near Negroes represent a change from their original attitudes.*

*Up to this point we are confident only that at least some "nears" have changed. Since we have no concrete knowledge of the absolute level of initial attitudes there remain two possibilities: that only "nears" have changed, or that more "nears" have changed than "fars." There is some evidence for the interpretation that some respondents living far from Negroes have changed as a result of experiences in the project; this will be dealt with in Chapters VI and VII.

Relative Influence of Proximity and Initial Attitude

IT NOW becomes possible to provide an answer to a basic question in studies of attitude change. If we grant that change has taken place for at least some respondents living near Negroes, it becomes desirable to ask who has undergone change. Is it only the initially favorable who now simply lose the last vestiges of bias? Or does the experience affect the originally unfavorable as well? Information on this question can be obtained in two ways: (1) by comparing, on each of the dependent variables, the present position of "nears" and "fars" roughly matched on the "index of estimated initial attitude"; and (2) by examining the respondents' own reports of *change* in attitude toward Negroes.

Comparison of Initially Similar "Nears" and "Fars"

Scores on the index of original disposition cannot, of course, be taken as indicating the absolute level of initial ethnic attitude, but simply as suggesting the likelihood of *more* favorable or *less* favorable initial attitude. Respondents occupying the "pro-Negro" position on *three or more items* were classified as having been originally "more favorable" toward Negroes; those occupying the "pro-Negro" position on *fewer than three items* were classified as originally "less favorable." In the following tables, the "more favorable" and "less favorable" respondents within each project are treated separately; within each of these categories the positions of "nears" and "fars" on each of the dependent variables are shown. In other words, this section will carry the earlier analysis a step further by comparing "nears" and "fars" when initial attitude is held reasonably constant. The tables may, of course, also be considered in another way. By examining, in addition, the responses of housewives who live the same distance from Negroes, but who differ in their initial attitudes, it is possible to estimate the *relative* influence of proximity and attitudinal predisposition. This will be done in the second major section of the chapter.

CONTACT WITH NEGROES IN THE PROJECT

As we have seen, white residents living near Negroes were much more likely than those living farther away to engage in neighborly activities with them and were much less likely than those living farther away to have no contact with Negroes or simply to greet them in passing. On the basis of the level of contact with Negroes, Table 28 compares the "nears" and "fars" among respondents who were classified as initially more favorable toward Negroes with the "nears" and "fars" classified as initially unfavorable. The table shows that proximity remains an important factor in determining the level of contact, whatever the individual's original disposition. In Integrated II, for example, among the initially more favorable, 35 per cent living in mixed buildings report neighborly association with Negroes, as compared with 18 per cent of those living in all-white buildings. The analogous proportions among the less favorably disposed respondents are 33 per cent of those in mixed buildings, 10 per cent of those in all-white buildings. The same regular proximity-group differences occur—whatever the original attitude—in the other three projects as well. At the other end of the scale, in every project strikingly fewer "nears" than "fars," among both the more favorably disposed and the less favorably disposed, report no contact whatsoever or at most casual greeting.*

ANTICIPATED REACTIONS OF FRIENDS IN THE PROJECT

It will be recalled that when initial disposition is not taken into account, white housewives living near Negroes are more likely than those living farther away to believe that their white friends in the project approve of friendly association with Negroes. Table 29 shows the responses to this question analyzed in terms of initial attitude as well as proximity. It is apparent that among the less favorably disposed in all four projects, and among the more favorably disposed in two projects, proximity is an important factor; those living near Negroes are more likely than those living farther away to believe that their friends are generally favorable to the idea of interracial association. In Building-Segregated I, for example, 55 per cent of the "nears" and 31 per cent of the "fars" among the more favorably disposed re-

---

*The finding of any "fars" at all who initially had less favorably disposed attitudes, but who nevertheless experience relatively intimate contact may occasion some surprise. We should note, however, that even the "fars" are probably living considerably nearer to Negroes than they were before they moved into the project. There may, in other words, be a proximity effect even for the "fars."

Table 28. Comparison between Proximity Groups on the Basis of Level of Contact, Initial Attitude Being Held Constant

Level of Contact with Negroes in Project	Integrated I				Building-Segregated I				Integrated II				Building-Segregated II			
	More Favorable		Less Favorable		More Favorable		Less Favorable		More Favorable		Less Favorable		More Favorable		Less Favorable	
	Near (32)	Far (47)	Near (41)	Far (60)	Near (38)	Far (51)	Near (39)	Far (44)	Near (34)	Far (51)	Near (79)	Far (94)	Near (29)	Far (57)	Near (29)	Far (81)
No contact	6%	15%	7%	30%	5%	20%	10%	48%	6%	37%	14%	50%	...	14%	4%	14%
Greets Negroes in casual street encounters	16	34	15	37	19	45	33	34	21	27	29	24	21%	41	31	50
Stops to talk in casual street encounters with Negroes	25	28	22	20	42	35	31	14	38	18	24	16	48	26	51	26
One or more kinds of neighborly activity	53	23	56	13	34	...	26	4	35	18	33	10	31	19	14	10

Table 29. Comparison between Proximity Groups on the Basis of Perception of the Social Climate, Initial Attitude Being Held Constant

Anticipated Reaction of White Friends in Project to Friendly Association with Negroes	Integrated I				Building-Segregated I				Integrated II				Building-Segregated II			
	More Favorable		Less Favorable		More Favorable		Less Favorable		More Favorable		Less Favorable		More Favorable		Less Favorable	
	Near (32)	Far (47)	Near (41)	Far (60)	Near (38)	Far (51)	Near (39)	Far (44)	Near (34)	Far (51)	Near (79)	Far (94)	Near (29)	Far (57)	Near (29)	Far (81)
Generally favorable	63%	66%	51%	37%	55%	31%	46%	16%	56%	37%	42%	18%	31%	26%	31%	22%
Mixed	3	6	7	...	3	10	3	4	...	4	4	...	...	4	10	1
Generally unfavorable	28	24	20	42	26	33	33	39	32	45	30	61	62	59	52	59
Don't know, not classifiable	6	4	22	21	16	26	18	41	12	14	24	21	7	11	7	18

port that their friends in the project approve of friendly association with Negroes; the analogous figures among the less favorably disposed are 46 per cent of "nears" and 16 per cent of "fars." In two projects, Integrated I and Building-Segregated II, there are no differences between proximity groups among the more favorably disposed; "nears" and "fars" anticipate almost identical reactions. It appears, then, that at least among white residents who were initially relatively unfavorable to Negroes, proximity to Negroes in the project is related to perception of the social climate as favorable or unfavorable to interracial contact.

FEELINGS ABOUT NEGROES IN THE PROJECT

Table 30 shows the proportions of "nears" and "fars" within each initial attitude grouping who expressed various degrees of "esteem" for the Negroes in the project. Here, as with level of contact, proximity-related differences appear among both the initially more favorable and the initially less favorable in all four projects. Whatever the initial attitude, respondents living near Negroes in the project are more likely to hold them in high esteem, and less likely to hold them in low esteem, than are those living farther away.

FEELINGS ABOUT LIVING WITH NEGROES

Table 31 compares "nears" and "fars" within the initial attitude groupings with respect to their feelings about living in a biracial project. Here again we find that regardless of initial attitude, white respondents who live near Negroes are less likely to disapprove of living in a mixed project than those who live farther away. The differences are not significant in every case, but the trend is consistent. In Integrated I, for example, among the more favorably disposed respondents, 28 per cent of those who lived in mixed buildings expressed *disapproval* of living in a biracial project, compared to 38 per cent of those who lived in all-white buildings. Among the less favorably disposed respondents in this same project, 42 per cent of those living in mixed buildings, compared to 60 per cent in all-white buildings, expressed disapproval of the biracial character of the project.

ATTITUDES TOWARD NEGROES IN GENERAL

Table 32 compares the scores on the Ethnocentrism Scale of "nears" and "fars" among the more favorably disposed and the less favorably disposed respondents. It will be remembered that five items were used, worded in such a way that agreement signified derogation of Negroes as a group; thus agreement with, at most, one item represents the least prejudiced position, agreement with four or five represents the most

Table 30. Comparison between Proximity Groups on the Basis of "Esteem" for Negroes in the Project, Initial Attitude Being Held Constant

Degree of Esteem	Integrated I				Building-Segregated I				Integrated II				Building-Segregated II			
	More Favorable		Less Favorable		More Favorable		Less Favorable		More Favorable		Less Favorable		More Favorable		Less Favorable	
	Near (32)	Far (47)	Near (41)	Far (60)	Near (38)	Far (51)	Near (39)	Far (44)	Near (34)	Far (51)	Near (79)	Far (94)	Near (29)	Far (57)	Near (29)	Far (81)
High	72%	51%	59%	35%	92%	53%	74%	30%	62%	43%	39%	26%	66%	60%	55%	43%
Mixed high and low	9	23	22	27	8	10	15	18	29	22	34	26	28	18	31	31
Low	19	26	17	38	...	29	8	41	9	31	27	42	3	19	10	25
Not classifiable	...	...	2	...	...	8	3	11	...	4	...	6	3	3	4	1

Table 31. Comparison between Proximity Groups on the Basis of Feelings about Living in a Negro-White Project, Initial Attitude Being Held Constant

Feeling	Integrated I				Building-Segregated I				Integrated II				Building-Segregated II			
	More Favorable		Less Favorable		More Favorable		Less Favorable		More Favorable		Less Favorable		More Favorable		Less Favorable	
	Near (32)	Far (47)	Near (41)	Far (60)	Near (38)	Far (51)	Near (39)	Far (44)	Near (34)	Far (51)	Near (79)	Far (94)	Near (29)	Far (57)	Near (29)	Far (81)
Approval	41%	24%	34%	17%	47%	38%	41%	30%	41%	29%	15%	12%	28%	32%	17%	21%
Mixed	31	36	24	22	45	25	38	25	18	14	14	15	45	25	41	30
Disapproval	28	38	42	60	5	25	21	41	41	57	68	70	24	40	42	43
Not classifiable	...	2	...	1	3	12	...	4	...	...	3	3	3	3	...	6

Table 32. Comparison between Proximity Groups on the Basis of the Amount of Agreement with Prejudiced Statements about Negroes in General, Initial Attitude Being Held Constant

Number of Items Agreed with*	Integrated I				Building-Segregated I				Integrated II				Building-Segregated II			
	More Favorable		Less Favorable		More Favorable		Less Favorable		More Favorable		Less Favorable		More Favorable		Less Favorable	
	Near (32)	Far (47)	Near (41)	Far (60)	Near (38)	Far (51)	Near (39)	Far (44)	Near (34)	Far (51)	Near (79)	Far (94)	Near (29)	Far (57)	Near (29)	Far (81)
At most 1	51%	30%	31%	22%	39%	37%	39%	23%	18%	12%	5%	3%	10%	18%	14%	11%
2 or 3	31	36	32	18	40	31	25	25	38	24	23	17	34	33	21	21
4 or 5	18	34	37	60	21	32	36	52	44	64	72	80	56	49	65	68

* Agreement indicates a negative attitude toward Negroes.

prejudiced. It can be seen from this table that in three of the projects, when we compare the respondents having the same initial attitude, the nearer to Negroes the white respondents live, the more likely they are to take a favorable view of Negroes in general. As an instance we may take Building-Segregated I. Among the more favorably disposed respondents in this project, 21 per cent of those living in mixed courts, compared to 32 per cent of those in all-white courts, took the most prejudiced position on the scale (that is, agreed with four or more items); among the less favorably disposed, 36 per cent of those in mixed courts, and 52 per cent of those in all-white courts, took the most prejudiced position. Similar differences between "nears" and "fars," whether initially relatively favorable or unfavorable, appeared in Integrated I and Integrated II. Only in Building-Segregated II did this relation not hold; it will be remembered that in this project there was no evidence of a relation between proximity and favorableness of general attitude toward Negroes even when initial attitude was not considered.

Influence of Initial Attitude

The comparisons presented in the preceding section permit the inference that, whatever their initial attitude, change has taken place at least for some respondents who live near Negroes. It is of special interest that there are sizeable effects of proximity on the level of contact, on perception of the norm favorable to interracial association, and on attitude, for those whose initial attitude was relatively *unfavorable*.

The data of Tables 28 through 32 make it possible to obtain answers to still another question: What is the influence of initial attitude on the dependent variables of the study? In other words, given a certain proximity to Negroes, are the initially less favorable as likely to undertake contact, to perceive the same social climate, and to hold the same ethnic attitudes as the initially more favorable?

Tables 28 and 29, dealing with the level of contact and the anticipated reactions of friends to interracial contact, provide an illustration of the interaction between proximity and initial attitude. Comparing the more favorably disposed and the less favorably disposed among the "nears" we find little systematic difference; among those who lived farther from Negroes, however, the differences related to initial attitude are more substantial.

Let us first consider Table 28. In Integrated I, for example, almost all the white residents who live *near* Negroes, regardless of initial attitude, have *some* contact with them; only 6 per cent of the more favorably disposed and 7 per cent of the less favorably disposed report no contact whatsoever. Among respondents living farther from Negroes the proportions reporting no contact are 15 per cent and 30 per cent respectively. A similar differential effect of initial attitude appears also in two of the remaining three projects.

This finding is not difficult to understand. As suggested in Chapter III, white residents who live close to Negroes are almost necessarily thrown into contact with them by the demands of everyday living; even those who are not disposed to seek out such contacts find them difficult to avoid. Those living farther away from Negroes in the project have greater freedom of choice in this respect. Their location neither demands nor prevents contact; thus there is opportunity for either seeking out contacts with Negroes or at least following up on those which occur by chance, if one is so inclined, or, on the other hand, for avoiding them without serious inconvenience. Under such circumstances initial disposition may be expected to play an important role.

Table 29 shows a similar situation with respect to the anticipated reactions of white friends in the project to the idea of interracial association. In three of the four projects initial attitude seems to play a smaller role among white women living near Negroes than among those living farther away. Thus, again considering Integrated I, we find among the "nears" 63 per cent of the more favorably disposed and 51 per cent of the less favorably disposed anticipating favorable reactions from friends in the project, a difference of 12 per cent. Among "fars" the parallel difference is 29 per cent. Only in Building-Segregated II does no relation—even among the "fars"—appear between initial disposition and anticipation of friends' reactions.

Here again it seems likely that the differential effects of initial attitude among "nears" and "fars" may be accounted for by differences in the objective situation. The white housewife who lives near Negroes, whatever her own initial attitude, sees interracial association taking place around her; she may even have more occasion to hear the question discussed, since neighborly contact with Negroes is a more real possibility for her and for her neighbors than for the housewife living farther away. The housewife living farther away, being less likely to observe interracial contact and thus having less objective evidence about the social climate, is somewhat freer to project her own feelings in response to a question about her friends' probable reactions to interracial association.

With respect to the less direct consequences, that is, the attitudinal measures, this particular pattern of interaction between proximity and initial attitude did not appear in our projects. Among "nears" as well as among "fars," respondents who initially were relatively favorably disposed toward Negroes were more favorable in attitude at the time of interviewing than were those who were initially less favorably disposed.

If we take Integrated II as an example, we see from Table 30 that among those living near Negroes, 62 per cent of the more favorably disposed, compared to 39 per cent of the less favorably disposed, now hold Negroes in the project in high esteem. Among those living farther from Negroes, a similar relation is found between initial attitude and present esteem; 43 per cent of the "fars" who were initially favorably disposed, compared to 26 per cent who were unfavorably disposed, now hold Negroes in the project in high esteem. Similar differences on this item are found among both "nears" and "fars" in the other projects, although in some cases the differences are less substantial.

Tables 31 and 32 also reveal that in either proximity group in a project, estimated initial attitude is related consistently to present feeling about living in a mixed project (Table 31) and to generalized attitudes (Table 32).

It is likely that the way in which the index of estimated initial attitude was constructed may have inflated the importance of the apparent role of initial attitude in determining the differences between "nears" and "fars" in present attitude. Items were selected for this index from a pool of items each of which was believed, on the basis of prior research, to be correlated with attitude toward Negroes. In the selection, however, those items were chosen which individually were most highly related to present attitude among the total group of respondents in each of the projects included in this study. It would be no surprise, therefore, if an index composed of such items should bear an exceptionally close relation to present attitude. If the influence of initial attitude *has* been exaggerated by this method of index construction it may be that in actuality, at least among "nears," a greater proportion change among the originally unfavorable than change among the originally more favorable. This appears possible since more of the former *can* change in a favorable direction; among the latter fewer can change since at least some already are at the most favorable point on the scale.

Respondents' Own Reports of Change in Attitude

The comparisons presented so far that permit the inference that attitude change has taken place for certain respondents have been based on estimates of probable initial attitudes drawn from the respondents' positions on a number of objective factors known to be generally correlated with ethnic attitudes. The discussion has been hampered by the fact that we had no precise knowledge of the initial attitude of an individual respondent and so have been unable to describe the extent of change in any individual. Now it is important to present evidence of another sort: the respondents' own evaluation of change in attitude toward Negroes. This is done in full recognition of the problems involved in self-evaluation of an earlier attitude and self-estimation of any change in that attitude.

During the interview the white respondents were asked the following questions: (1) Before you moved into the project, what did you think colored people were like, from what you had heard or read or just felt, or from your experience? (2) Since living in this project, would you say your feelings or ideas about colored people have changed quite a lot, a little, or not at all? (If changed "quite a lot" or "a little": 3) Have your feelings or ideas about colored people changed for the better or for the worse?

As has already been shown in Table 26, there were no very striking differences between "nears" and "fars" in any of the four projects in their reported impressions of Negroes before moving into the project.

The white respondents' evaluations of their *changes* in attitude toward Negroes are shown in Table 33. In each project, at least two-fifths of the housewives living near Negroes and about one-quarter living farther away report that since living in the project their attitude toward Negroes has changed for the better, with consistent and significant differences between proximity groups in every project. In Integrated II, for example, 43 per cent of the white respondents living in mixed Negro-white buildings report that their attitudes toward Negroes have changed for the better, compared to 22 per cent of the respondents in all-white buildings.

The table gives striking evidence that the proximity of the white respondent to Negroes in the project is related to her own perception of change in attitude toward them. Not only do we have confirmation

Table 33. Differences between Proximity Groups on the Basis of Self-Reported Changes in Attitude toward Negroes

Change in Attitude	Integrated I Near (73)	Integrated I Far (107)	Building-Segregated I Near (77)	Building-Segregated I Far (95)	Integrated II Near (113)	Integrated II Far (145)	Building-Segregated II Near (58)	Building-Segregated II Far (138)
For the better ...	60%	32% *	41%	22% *	43%	22% *	48%	27% *
For the worse ...	4	7	...	1	5	10	5	3
No change	34	61	59	77	51	68	45	69
No answer	2	...	...	...	1	...	2	1

* Differences are significant at least at the .05 level of confidence as calculated by the *t* test for significance of differences between percentages.

of our previous inferences regarding attitude change among the "nears" but for the first time have evidence regarding change among the "fars." However, it is obvious that change in attitude is not a meaningful measurement unless there is some base-line from which it can be gauged. As such a base-line, we have the white respondent's report of her impressions of Negroes before she moved into the project. Given similar initial reactions, are there differences between "nears" and "fars" in reported change in attitude toward Negroes?

Table 34 shows separately the reported attitude change of those whose original impressions were *unfavorable,* and of those whose original impressions were favorable or neutral. Those who reported their original impression of Negroes as predominantly *unfavorable* provide the most important information on the relationship between change in attitude and proximity to Negroes in the project, since in this originally unfavorable group there was the greatest possibility for attitude change to take place. In each proximity group in all projects those who were originally unfavorable were at least twice as likely as those originally favorable or neutral to report that their attitudes have *changed for the better.*

Moreover, in all four projects, without exception, among the white respondents who reported their prior attitudes as *unfavorable,* those who now live near Negroes in the project are much more likely than those who live farther away to report that their attitudes have *changed for the better.* For example, in Integrated I, of the white respondents whose reported prior impressions were unfavorable, 82 per cent of those who live in mixed Negro-white buildings report that they have changed in attitude for the better, as compared to 43 per cent who live in all-white buildings; only 18 per cent of those in mixed buildings, as compared to 53 per cent of those in all-white buildings, report *no* change in attitude.

A white respondent in Integrated II who lived next door to a Negro family provides an example of those with originally unfavorable impressions who reported change for the better. This respondent described her attitude toward Negroes before she moved into the project in this way: "I thought they were hard to get along with. I was actually afraid of them—always fighting with the whites, ready to knife them, not to be trusted." She reported that since living in the project her feelings and ideas about Negroes had changed for the better: "They [Negroes] are not so bad; there are good and bad amongst both [races]. The family who lived next door here was always very clean and always ready to help us; [the Negro housewife] always asked if she could do me a little favor." In Building-Segregated I, a white respondent who lived near

Table 34. Relation between Proximity and Changes in Attitude toward Negroes, Based on Self-Reports of Prior and Present Attitudes

Reported Change in Attitude	Integrated I		Building-Segregated I		Integrated II		Building-Segregated II	
	Near	Far	Near	Far	Near	Far	Near	Far
Percentage of Respondents Having Unfavorable Prior Impression								
	(N = 38)	(N = 55)	(N = 29)	(N = 35)	(N = 70)	(N = 81)	(N = 29)	(N = 47)
For the better	82%	48%*	79%	43%*	56%	28%*	86%	49%*
For the worse	...	4	...	3	4	9	...	2
No change	18	53	21	54	40	63	14	49
Percentage of Respondents Having Favorable or Neutral Prior Impression								
	(N = 33)	(N = 49)	(N = 45)	(N = 56)	(N = 37)	(N = 61)	(N = 28)	(N = 82)
For the better	36	18	13	7	19	13	11	13
For the worse	12	8	...	...	8	13	14	4
No change	52	74	87	93	73	74	75	83
Number of Respondents Not Classifiable by Prior Impression								
Indeterminable	2	3	3	4	6	3	1	9

* Differences are significant at least at the .05 level of confidence as calculated by the *t* test for significance of differences between percentages.

Negroes also reported an originally unfavorable attitude: "I thought they were not neat or clean, not too intelligent, and rather loud and inclined to fight." Since living in the project, she said, "I've found my first impressions were all wrong. Colored people can be just as nice for friends: neat, clean, quiet, fine neighbors." Concerning what caused her to change her feelings or ideas about Negroes, she said, "Just from my observation by casual meeting on the street—and this isn't very often."

It may be noted from Table 34 that substantial proportions of white respondents living relatively far from Negroes reported having changed for the better from an originally unfavorable attitude. The respondents in this category range from about one-quarter of the "fars" in Integrated II, to about one-half the "fars" in Building-Segregated II. However, because those who live relatively far from Negroes are less likely to have contact with them, it may be anticipated that "change for the better" reported by them actually means *less* change than a similar report would from those who live near Negroes. The relative amount of change undergone by "nears" and "fars" can be gauged by comparing the two groups in terms of the present level of "esteem" for Negroes in the project, limiting the comparison to those who were originally unfavorable and report that they have changed for the better. If the white respondents who live farther away have changed *as much as* those living near Negroes, then the proportions of the two groups at the various levels of esteem should be similar. That this is by no means the case, however, is shown by Table 35. Among the white respondents who reported their prior impressions to be *unfavorable* and who also reported that they had *changed for the better,* a greater proportion of those living near Negroes than of those living farther away now express

Table 35. Relation between Proximity and "Esteem" for Negroes among Respondents Reporting Originally Unfavorable Impressions and Subsequent Change for the Better

Degree of Esteem Now Reported	Integrated I		Building-Segregated I		Integrated II		Building-Segregated II	
	Near (31)	Far (24)	Near (23)	Far (15)	Near (39)	Far (23)	Near (25)	Far (23)
High	69%	38%	79%	20%	48%	31%	64%	57%
Mixed high and low	19	16	17	20	39	35	24	17
Low	12	46	4	46	13	34	8	26
Not classifiable ..	...	...	...	14	...	...	4	...
χ^2	7.7		14.3		4.5		3.1	
d.f.	2		2		2		2	
p	<.05		<.01		<.10		>.10	

high esteem for the Negroes in the project. These results suggest that living near Negroes rather than far from them makes it not only more likely that a larger proportion will report a favorable change in attitude but also that whatever change does take place is *greater in extent.*

Summary

Comparisons based on initial attitudes as estimated from a number of objective factors reveal the powerful influence of proximity regardless of initial attitude. Whether we consider the initially more favorable or initially less favorable respondents, those who live near Negroes in a project are more likely than those living farther away to report neighborly contact, to anticipate that white friends in the project will approve of such contact, to have high esteem for the Negroes in the project, to approve of the biracial aspect of the project, and to have a favorable attitude toward Negroes in general. These "near"-"far" differences may be interpreted as reflecting change in attitude at least for "nears." It is of interest to note that such changes take place even among those with an initially less favorable attitude.

The basic findings regarding "nears" are confirmed by respondents' own reports of the change they sense in themselves since living in the projects. Thus, no fewer than half the "nears" in each project who had unfavorable impressions of Negroes before moving into the project reported changing in a favorable direction.

These self-evaluations also reveal that a substantial number of "fars" with unfavorable initial impressions of Negroes also underwent favorable change, although the proportions changing were in every case much smaller than among "nears" in the same projects. Further analysis showed that "nears" reporting change were considerably more likely to put Negroes in the highest category of "esteem" than were "fars" who reported similar change, suggesting that the *amount of change* is more marked among "nears."

The data indicate that close proximity to Negroes tends to outweigh initial attitude in its effect upon interracial contact and the white resident's perception of the social climate regarding such contact. Regardless of the housewife's personal inclination, the requirements of everyday living make it almost certain that, if she lives close to Negroes in the project, she will have *some* contact with them, and furthermore make it likely that this contact will extend beyond mere greeting. The housewife who lives near Negroes is also likely, whatever her original attitude, to perceive that other white women around her approve of interracial association.

However, initial attitude was also found to play a substantial role in determining present attitude. While self-evaluations of changes in attitude indicate that a higher proportion of the initially unfavorable change in a positive direction than do the initially favorable, the originally less favorable seemed somewhat less likely to report favorable attitudes at the time of interviewing.

CHAPTER VII

Contact, Social Climate, and Attitudes

In the preceding chapters we have demonstrated a series of discrete relationships between proximity, on the one hand, and three sets of variables—contact, social climate, and ethnic attitude—on the other. It now becomes desirable to examine the interrelationships remaining among these three sets of variables when the effects of proximity per se have been eliminated.

We have, for instance, shown that proximity is related to more intimate contact, and we have shown that proximity is related to more favorable attitudes. We might be tempted to infer that we have already demonstrated that more frequent and more intimate contact leads to more favorable attitudes. It is conceivable, however, that proximity may be related to extent of contact, and that proximity may be related to high "esteem," but that high "esteem" may not be directly related to contact. Or that proximity may be related to the perceived social climate without the latter's being related in any direct way to attitude. In other words, we do not yet know on the basis of the data reviewed up to now whether proximity per se is the responsible agent for the changes in attitude or whether proximity leads to increased contact and changes in perceived social climate, and these in turn to changes in attitude.

We can approach this problem by looking separately at each degree of proximity and determining for each whether or not contact and perceived social climate are still related to attitudes. This approach requires a different breakdown of the data; and in order to preserve enough cases in the comparison groups, the findings for the two integrated projects will be considered together, as will those for the two segregated projects.

Contact and Attitude

Let us examine the attitudes of white residents toward Negroes in relation to the amount of interracial contact they have in the project.

Table 36. Relation between Level of Contact and Degree of "Esteem"
for Negroes in the Project

Degree of Esteem	Near			Far		
	Neighborly Activity (Visiting, etc.)	Extended Street Conversation	No Contacts beyond Casual Greeting	Neighborly Activity (Visiting, etc.)	Extended Street Conversation	No Contacts beyond Casual Greeting
Percentage of Respondents in Integrated I and II (Combined)						
	(N = 78)	(N = 49)	(N = 59)	(N = 37)	(N = 49)	(N = 165)
High	74%	45%	32%	49%	45%	31%
Mixed high and low	22	33	27	38	33	19
Low	4	22	39	13	22	45
Not classifiable. ...		...	2	...	...	5
Percentage of Respondents in Building-Segregated I and II (Combined)						
	(N = 36)	(N = 57)	(N = 42)	(N = 21)	(N = 60)	(N = 152)
High	85%	75%	59%	57%	64%	38%
Mixed high and low	12	21	24	29	22	19
Low	3	2	12	14	12	36
Not classifiable. ...		2	5	...	2	7

Table 36 shows this relationship for those living near Negroes and for those living farther away. In the integrated projects, 32 per cent of the white housewives living near Negroes and having no contact with them beyond casual greetings hold them in high esteem, compared to 45 per cent of those engaging in street conversations and 74 per cent of those having apartment-centered contact. Among all women living far from Negroes in the same projects the proportions holding Negroes in high esteem are 31, 45, and 49 per cent respectively.

Before proceeding to the interpretation of the role of contact in bringing about attitude change, it is well to consider the influence of initial attitudes on the data of Table 36. We could, in fact, under certain circumstances, expect a similar finding to that shown in the tables even if extent of contact were unrelated to attitude change. We have already shown, for example, that among "fars" the initially more favorably disposed respondents were in general more likely to take part in conversational and neighborly interracial contacts than were those initially less favorably disposed. Other findings have revealed that those initially more favorably disposed were also more likely to hold the most favorable present attitudes. Thus, it is possible that some of the relationships occurring in Table 36 may be attributable to the relationship between initial attitude and contact.

In order to assess the role of the contact experience, therefore, it seems desirable to examine separately the relation between contact and present attitude for the initially more and the initially less favorably disposed white housewives, making use, again, of the "index of estimated initial attitude." Table 37 shows the relation between contact and four separate attitude items (each presented in abbreviated fashion) for those white women characterized as originally less favorably disposed toward Negroes, and for those originally more favorably disposed. In reading the table it should be noted that for simplicity of presentation the two levels of closest contact have been combined. Table 37 tells us that whether we consider the housewives who were initially more favorably or those who were initially less favorably disposed, the more intimate their contact the more favorable their attitude. This is true for all categories of respondents, integrated or building-segregated, whether living near Negroes or farther away. Each of the thirty-two comparisons made in the two parts of the table shows a difference in the expected direction.

For example, among the housewives characterized as initially less favorably disposed who live near Negroes in the integrated projects (first half of Table 37), 28 per cent more of those with conversational or neighborly contacts than those with no contact beyond casual greeting hold Negroes in high esteem; 18 per cent more believe the races are equal on at least two characteristics, 34 per cent more take less prejudiced positions on the scale of generalization, and 37 per cent more approve, in some way, of living in a Negro-white project. The lower part of Table 37 shows parallel differences among the housewives who are similarly situated but who were initially more favorably disposed. It thus seems clear that for the women living near Negroes such attitude change as has taken place in the projects has occurred at least in part through the mediation of the contact experience.

Examining the findings for the white women living *far* from Negroes in both kinds of projects, we see that contact is also markedly related to attitudes. The more intimate the contact, the more favorable the attitude—without exception.

These data help to account for the differences in ethnic attitude which have been shown to be related to proximity. While contact is related to attitude within proximity groups (both in the "near" group and in the "far" group) as we have just indicated, the fact is that a considerably greater proportion of the population of "nears" than of "fars" have interracial contact beyond casual greeting. The significance of this finding is that at any level of initial disposition there is a considerably greater proportion of "nears" than "fars" who have at least

Table 37. Relation between Contact and Attitude among the Initially Less and the Initially More Favorably Disposed

Attitude	Integrated I and II (Combined)				Building-Segregated I and II (Combined)			
	Near		Far		Near		Far	
	Conversational or Neighborly Contacts	No Contact beyond Casual Greeting	Conversational or Neighborly Contacts	No Contact beyond Casual Greeting	Conversational or Neighborly Contacts	No Contact beyond Casual Greeting	Conversational or Neighborly Contacts	No Contact beyond Casual Greeting
Percentage among Housewives Initially Less Favorably Disposed								
	(N = 77)	(N = 43)	(N = 44)	(N = 110)	(N = 41)	(N = 27)	(N = 37)	(N = 88)
High "esteem"	56%	28%	41%	25%	76%	52%	59%	30%
Belief in equality of Negroes and whites on at least 2 items of scale	88	70	73	55	90	81	86	51
Agreement with at most 3 items of generalized attitude scale	52	18	44	22	58	41	46	35
Approval of living in Negro-white projects (qualified and unqualified)	53	16	48	25	73	67	70	44
Percentage among Housewives Initially More Favorably Disposed								
	(N = 50)	(N = 16)	(N = 42)	(N = 56)	(N = 52)	(N = 15)	(N = 44)	(N = 64)
High "esteem"	74%	43%	52%	42%	82%	73%	66%	50%
Belief in equality of Negroes and whites on at least 2 items of scale	86	69	83	61	88	80	82	67
Agreement with at most 3 items of generalized attitude scale	74	51	64	39	64	53	70	51
Approval of living in Negro-white projects (qualified and unqualified)	74	38	65	41	84	80	75	48

conversational contacts with Negroes *and* more favorable attitudes toward them.

The evidence seems conclusive that contact is related to favorable attitude change. Can we say that relatively intimate contact has *caused* the more favorable attitudes? Speculation about the process which takes place in the interaction of these factors suggests that the process may be circular and that contact may be viewed as both cause and effect of favorable attitude change.

For the originally hostile white woman, initial interracial contacts are likely at first to be casual. As her contacts with Negroes continue to the conversational stage, there are likely to be incremental changes in beliefs, feelings, and policy orientation. As the white housewife becomes more favorably disposed, the hindrances to still higher levels of contact diminish, making such contacts more and more likely. Upon repetition of the activity, the change which has already taken place is reinforced and then extended. The relationship between contact and attitude modification would thus be seen to be similar to that which is characteristic of all social *processes,* a dynamic interaction among the components. Attitude is not the only aspect of this process that undergoes change in the course of time; presumably, the nature of the contact changes as well.

This account of the relationship between developing contact and developing attitude seems congruent with the data presented thus far, and appears equally applicable to the initially more and the initially less hostile white women. Those beginning with more favorable attitudes are less likely at the outset to resist preliminary casual interaction with Negroes when opportunity presents itself. Here again, our view is that increments of contact give rise to increments of favorable attitude, which in reciprocating fashion make more likely repeated and increasingly intimate contact. Since these women start at a high level of favorable attitude position, the contact-attitude process culminates at a level even higher than that of some of the initially less favorably disposed women who have similar contacts.

The analysis suggests that for many respondents, the level of contact reached determines the extent to which attitude is changed. Many factors may contribute to limiting contacts to less intimate levels and so to preventing attitude from changing maximally. For example, some white women or the Negro women who live near them work, so that extended interracial contact is relatively unfeasible. Other possible participants in more intimate Negro-white contacts suffer illness and are confined to the house. In other cases, differences in age, background, and interests between white and Negro women who live near one an-

other inhibit the development of further contacts. It is also possible
that initially unfavorable attitudes may limit the development of contacts. Still another factor is one whose influences we shall examine in
the following section: the perceived climate of opinion regarding the
social permissibility of interracial contacts.

Perceived Social Climate and Attitude

The theory underlying this study holds that prejudice is in large part
learned from and supported by existing social arrangements which
bespeak disapproval of association between the races. In the projects of
the present study, several of the elements ordinarily discouraging to
Negro-white interaction seem to be absent. To begin with there is the
fact that Negroes *do* live in the projects and, in general, without clear-
cut separation between the races. It may be recalled that only a very
small proportion of the white housewives, whatever their distance from
Negroes, felt that the project management was against racial interaction. Another and perhaps equally potent influence regarding the
permissibility of racial interaction is the anticipated reaction of white
friends in the project regarding this issue. As we have seen, there is a
tendency for the "nears" more than for the "fars" to anticipate that
their friends will have favorable reactions.

What is the relation between anticipated reaction of friends and
ethnic attitude? When we examine the attitudes of the white housewives in the light of the different reactions they anticipate from their
friends, we find for all attitude variables a direct relationship: the more
favorable the anticipation the more favorable the attitude. Table 38
gives the data for the respondents initially less favorably disposed and
for those initially more favorably disposed. As before, four comparisons are made in each half of the table on each of four attitude items.
The two parts of the table together show thirty-two comparisons between respondents who are equated as to initial attitude but who differ in their interpretation of the social permissibility of being friendly
with Negroes. Each of the comparisons reveals the same trend. As in
the comparable tables relating contact and attitude, the relationship
applies to housewives who live relatively far from Negroes as well as
to those who live relatively near.

A question now arises as to the *meaning* of the perception of social
climate as favorable or unfavorable to interracial association. Does the
housewife's estimate of her friends' reactions represent simply a
rationalization of her own behavior or of her own attitudes? Or is there
a tendency for the white housewife to select white friends whose attitudes are like her own?

Table 38. Relation between Perception of the Social Climate and Attitude among the Initially Less and the Initially More Favorably Disposed

Attitude	Integrated I and II (Combined)				Building-Segregated I and II (Combined)			
	Near		Far		Near		Far	
	Favorable Perception	Unfavorable Perception	Favorable Perception	Unfavorable Perception	Favorable Perception	Unfavorable Perception	Favorable Perception	Unfavorable Perception
	Percentage among Housewives Initially Less Favorably Disposed							
	(N = 50)	(N = 32)	(N = 36)	(N = 82)	(N = 25)	(N = 28)	(N = 23)	(N = 65)
High "esteem"	56%	22%	42%	17%	88%	43%	48%	35%
Belief in equality of Negroes and whites on at least 2 items of scale	88	81	83	55	92	89	78	63
Agreement with at most 3 items of generalized attitude scale	44	25	47	22	60	43	44	25
Approval of living in Negro-white projects (qualified and unqualified)	50	22	50	20	92	43	65	40
	Percentage among Housewives Initially More Favorably Disposed							
	(N = 37)	(N = 20)	(N = 46)	(N = 34)	(N = 30)	(N = 28)	(N = 27)	(N = 51)
High "esteem"	78%	45%	57%	29%	93%	60%	75%	45%
Belief in equality of Negroes and whites on at least 2 items of scale	86	75	74	59	93	86	85	78
Agreement with at most 3 items of generalized attitude scale	76	55	66	44	87	36	63	55
Approval of living in Negro-white projects (qualified and unqualified)	70	50	68	27	94	71	63	58

Each of these possibilities is likely to apply to some of the white women in the project; our data do not permit singling out those who fit each of the possibilities. However, there is some indication that a number of the white residents based their perception of the social climate on more or less objective evidence which was independent of their own behavior. Thus, several items point to the interpretation that our white respondents' view of the social climate—their anticipation of friends' reactions—is based to a considerable degree on the inferences they draw from the Negro-white interaction going on around them which they have daily opportunity to observe. Some evidence may be gathered from the respondents' reports of *mingling* which takes place between white and Negro women in the project. The observation of contact between white and Negro housewives may be thought of as somewhat less open to distortion than the estimate of friends' attitudes. The relationship between observation of interracial mingling and anticipation of friends' reaction is very high. For example, considering the four projects together, more than four-fifths among those anticipating unfavorable reactions *do not* report perceiving interracial mingling.

Evidence suggesting that the perception of social climate is independent of the white resident's own behavior is provided by a comparison of the respondent's own level of contact and her estimate of her friends' probable reaction to interracial association. If the perception of social climate were dictated primarily by rationalization of one's own contact experience, there should be a high proportion of respondents whose reports on these two points are in the same direction; that is, there should be a predominance of women who report either high contact and favorable reaction of friends or low contact and unfavorable reactions of friends.* Our data, however, show that this is not the case. Only a little more than half the respondents in any project (and less than half in two of the projects) showed such concordance between their own level of contact and their anticipation of friends' reactions to interracial association. The conclusion seems justified, then, that perception of social climate is based on more or less objective evidence and that the perception of favorable or unfavorable social climate is related to degree of "esteem" for Negroes in the project, independently of one's own contact with them. This interpretation clearly corresponds to the comment of a white respondent in Building-Segregated I who said: "At first . . . I was afraid of what other whites would do. I hung back waiting to see what others did."

---

* Even if every respondent who had conversational contact viewed the social climate as favorable and everyone who did not have such contact viewed the social climate as unfavorable, the relationship between the two variables need not necessarily be attributed to rationalization of one's own behavior.

What are the possible interpretations of the findings described in this section? One reasonable interpretation is that many women in the project, originally hostile toward Negroes—or, at best, not completely favorable—have had their attitudes shaped by the apparent social acceptability of Negro-white association in the project. It is possible that perception of a climate favorable to racial interaction cuts down impediments to one's own contacts with Negroes, and with developing contacts comes appreciation of Negroes as human beings with good and bad qualities. Or that even when contact itself does not develop, for whatever reasons, the perception of a favorable social climate may of itself promote favorable beliefs, feelings, and policy orientations regarding Negroes who seem to be generally accepted and may possibly be known to be friends of friends.

Precisely what it is that convinces some white women that friendly interaction is permissible and other white women that it is not is of course difficult to say. One may be so occupied with her own affairs, either inside or outside the project, that she really hasn't had a chance to find out the true state of affairs. Another may interpret the social climate as unfavorable because her immediate circle of friends happens to be resistant to interracial friendliness. Accidents of placement or of activity in the project may make the converse true for some. A white woman who regularly suns her baby outside the house on a busy street in the project may be in a better position to perceive many instances of interracial friendliness in the course of a day. Similarly, membership in a friendship group *not* hostile to interaction may enhance the likelihood of the white resident's inference about favorable social climate. Whatever influences the perceptual process, the fact remains that its end result is related to attitude.

Interrelation between Contact, Social Climate, and Attitude

Since contact and social climate have been found separately to be related to attitude, it is now desirable to explore the consequences of their interaction. Table 39 presents the data necessary to do this. The data in this table do not include a breakdown in terms of the initially more and the initially less favorably disposed because the number of respondents becomes so small that percentages are no longer meaningful. It suffices to say that even with the additional breakdown the results are consistent with the data in the table (i.e., the directions of the differences are the same when the initially favorably and unfavorably disposed are considered separately).

In each half of the table there are two proximity groups which we are evaluating on each of the four attitude items. In fourteen out of

Table 39. Interrelation between Contact, Perception of the Social Climate, and Attitude, in Integrated I and II (Combined) and in Building-Segregated I and II (Combined)

	Near				Far			
	Conversational or Neighborly Contacts		No Contact beyond Casual Greeting		Conversational or Neighborly Contacts		No Contact beyond Casual Greeting	
Attitude	Favorable Perception	Unfavorable Perception	Favorable Perception	Unfavorable Perception	Favorable Perception	Unfavorable Perception	Favorable Perception	Unfavorable Perception
	Percentage among Housewives in Integrated I and II (Combined)							
	(N = 69)	(N = 28)	(N = 18)	(N = 24)	(N = 46)	(N = 26)	(N = 30)	(N = 90)
High "esteem"	74%	39%	33%	21%	50%	35%	50%	17%
Belief in equality of Negroes and whites on at least 2 items of scale	93	79	67	79	83	73	72	51
Agreement with at most 3 items of generalized attitude scale	67	43	22	29	67	39	41	26
Approval of living in Negro-white projects (qualified and unqualified)	71	48	12	21	63	38	56	17
	Percentage among Housewives in Building-Segregated I and II (Combined)							
	(N = 40)	(N = 38)	(N = 15)	(N = 18)	(N = 17)	(N = 47)	(N = 33)	(N = 69)
High "esteem"	92%	60%	87%	34%	82%	45%	52%	36%
Belief in equality of Negroes and whites on at least 2 items of scale	90	89	100	83	88	83	79	61
Agreement with at most 3 items of generalized attitude scale	77	47	67	45	71	56	45	26
Approval of living in Negro-white projects (qualified and unqualified)	92	63	93	51	70	66	61	37

106

the sixteen comparisons,* the *most* favorable attitudes are held by white housewives who have at least conversational contacts *and* who perceive the social climate as favorable to interracial association. In thirteen out of the sixteen comparisons, the *least* favorable attitudes are held by respondents who neither have conversational contact nor view the social climate as favorable.

Falling between these two extreme groups were two other groups of respondents: those who had at least conversational contact with Negroes but perceived the social climate as unfavorable, and those who had less than conversational contact but who perceived the social climate as favorable. In all sixteen of the comparisons at least one of these groups fell between the extremes in attitude; and in eleven of the comparisons, this was true of both groups.

The differences between the two extreme groups are in most cases quite marked. For example, among "nears" in the integrated projects, 74 per cent of those with both contact and perceived social climate operating in the "positive" direction hold Negroes in high "esteem," compared to 21 per cent of those with the two factors working in the "negative" direction, a difference of 53 per cent. If we average the corresponding percentages on the "high esteem" item for the "nears" and "fars" in both kinds of projects, the difference between the both-factors-favorable and the both-factors-unfavorable groups is 47 per cent; similarly, the difference between these averages on the "generalized attitude" item is 39 per cent, and for "approval of living in Negro-white projects" the difference is again 47 per cent. For the item "belief in equality" the difference between the average of the extreme contact–social-climate groups is considerably smaller, 17 per cent.

In general, then, although there are several exceptions, contact and the perceived social climate tend to reinforce each other when their influence operates in the same direction† and to cancel each other out when their influence works in opposite directions. The exceptions are of considerable interest since they throw light on the *relative* influence of contact and the perceived social climate in affecting attitudes.

* We are referring here to the comparisons within the project-proximity groups (e.g., the "nears" in the integrated projects). Since there are four project-proximity groups and four attitude items, there are sixteen comparisons (the first four figures in any row constituting one such comparison, and the last four another). Many other comparisons are possible with the data in these tables. The comparisons we are making have the effect of holding type of project and distance relatively constant within each comparison.

† The reasons for the more favorable present attitudes among "nears" than among "fars," as reported in Chapter IV, become even clearer at this point. The proportion of women with both conversational contacts *and* favorable perceived climate was considerably greater among "nears" than among "fars." Conversely the proportion of women with only casual greeting *and* unfavorable perceived climate was considerably greater among "fars" than among "nears."

Among "fars" in integrated and building-segregated projects alike, no consistent trend emerges suggesting the primacy of one or another of the variables as an influence on attitude. At relatively great distance from Negroes in the project, if the white housewife is "positive" on *only one* of the two variables, it makes little difference whether she is positive on one or the other: she is equally likely to be favorable or unfavorable in attitude.

There does however, appear to be a systematic difference between the groups of "nears" in the two kinds of projects. Among "nears" in the integrated projects (top half of Table 39), contact appears more strikingly related to favorable attitude than does the social climate. For respondents with less than conversational contact, for example, the social climate appears to make little or no difference, and when respondents are compared who are "positive" on either contact or social climate (but not on both), a greater proportion of those with high contact have favorable attitudes than of those perceiving only a favorable social climate; the average difference on the four items is almost 20 per cent.

The converse is true among the building-segregated "nears" (bottom half of Table 39). Here perceived social climate appears as the more significant variable. When we consider respondents with the same level of contact, those perceiving a favorable climate are considerably more likely to hold favorable attitudes than those perceiving an unfavorable social climate. The average difference due to perceived social climate is almost 30 per cent. However, holding social climate constant, contact is shown to play a lesser role; the average difference due to contact is only about 10 per cent.

One explanation of the differential role of contact and perceived social climate between the "nears" in the two kinds of projects is related to the nature of the contacts taking place in each. "Conversational or neighborly contacts" embraces both the relatively more intimate neighborly visiting as well as street-centered conversational contacts, the two categories having been combined in this chapter for simplicity of presentation. It will be recalled from Chapter III that about 40 per cent of the "nears" in integrated projects had the more intimate neighborly contacts, compared to about 25 per cent of the "nears" in the building-segregated projects. The relatively greater influence of contact for integrated "nears" may be attributed to the greater prevalence of the more intimate "neighborly" contacts among these respondents. In the building-segregated projects, with fewer conversational contacts occurring in the context of "neighborly" visiting, the influence of the perceived social climate emerges more fully.

Before concluding the discussion of the interrelation between contact, perception of the social climate, and attitude, it is worth while to draw attention to a point that may have theoretical and practical importance: the fact that the perceived social climate is related to attitude even for respondents who have no contact with Negroes beyond casual greeting. Table 39 reveals that among such respondents those who perceive the social climate as favorable to contact are somewhat more likely to have favorable attitudes than are those who perceive the social climate as unfavorable. This relationship holds in three of the four "casual greeting" groups presented. Only among "nears" in the integrated projects when no more than casual contact occurs, are the differences between the two social climate groups small and inconsistent.

It is difficult from our data to answer decisively the question of the relative influence of contact and perceived social climate. However, the findings of this chapter have helped to specify what appear to be major factors in attitude change—the level of interracial contact reached and an awareness of the informal social pressures promoting or hindering interracial contact. In line with our previous discussion, it is doubtful whether either of these factors can be said to *cause* attitude change. Instead they are likely to interact with each other and with attitude, each developing until some sort of stability is reached.

The Process of Growing Acquaintance and Attitude Change

Moving into a housing project open to both white and Negro tenants, the white housewife enters a community in which society's restrictions causing marked separation between the races appear to be suspended. She now lives closer to Negroes than she ever has before. These Negro families are, moreover, by virtue of rental policy, likely to be similar to her own family in many important ways. Depending on her location in the project and typical activities that necessitate her going in and out of her apartment, there is a characteristic range of possibilities for initial encounters with Negro residents and a characteristic range of possible observations of the encounters between the same Negroes and other white women.

As time goes on, if she lives near enough to Negro residents to pass them in the street or to do her work or spend leisure time while Negro women similarly engaged are near by, she is likely to have a nodding acquaintance with them. The course of events from this point on is a function of many other factors, some systematic and some fortuitous.

Whether her interracial contact develops in the direction of intimacy may be dependent upon such factors as initial attitudes (especially so for those living great distances from Negroes), ethnic attitudes of friends in white friendship groups inside and outside the project, customary out-of-the-house activities, similarities or differences in background, age, interests, age of children, etc., between herself and the Negro women she has casual contact with, the attitudes of these same Negroes toward the developing contact with whites, and so on.

At what point the process of attitude change is begun is difficult to say from the data of this study. It may begin during the early casual meetings when the white housewife encounters Negroes not true to stereotype and notes this fact. Possibly it may begin when she learns from early observation of or personal conversations with Negroes that their aims, aspirations, and problems are a good deal like her own. Or it may begin only when she realizes from her own observations and from conversations with white friends that relatively intimate behavior with Negroes is behavior acceptable to other white people.

Whatever the point at which change is instigated, changing attitude is likely to influence and then, in turn, be influenced by the developing contact, in reciprocating fashion. Both contact and attitude are affected by the reaction to the perceived informal pressures facilitating or discouraging continued contact. In the event that more than casual contact is feasible, a favorable perceived climate probably plays a significant role in its taking place and thus lays the groundwork for the development of the most favorable attitudes. However, even where more intimate contact is not feasible for a number of possible reasons, the knowledge or feeling that white friends in the project are not against interracial contact permits the continuation of the process of change already begun.

Level of interracial contact and the anticipated reactions of friends regarding that contact are not the only factors involved in the process of attitude change, nor are the details of this process involving the two factors understood in all possible variations. However, deriving from the basic hypotheses of the study and congruent with the data, the preceding conceptualization provides a way of accounting for the attitude changes that have taken place for many white residents since living in the project.

Summary

It appears that contact with Negroes and the perception of the social climate with regard to interracial association, both independently and in interaction, influence ethnic attitude. Whether we consider the originally more or less favorably disposed, the basic data are the same: more intimate contact and a favorable perception of the social climate are each related to favorable attitude. Those who themselves have relatively intimate contacts with Negroes, and who perceive the social atmosphere as approving of such contacts, are likely to express the highest "esteem" for Negroes in the project, are more likely to believe that Negroes and whites are equal in a number of characteristics, are less likely to hold generalized prejudiced views of Negroes, and are more likely to express approval of living in a Negro-white project. At the other extreme, those who themselves have at most superficial contact with Negroes and who perceive the social climate as unfavorable to closer association, are the least likely to hold Negroes in the project in high "esteem," etc. Thus the hypotheses with respect to the influence of contact and of perceived social climate on ethnic attitude are supported.

The finding that contact and the perceived social climate are directly related to attitude helps to account for the differences in attitude between proximity groups found in earlier chapters. A far greater proportion of women living near Negroes than of those living farther away have conversational contact with Negroes and interpret the social climate as favorable to contact. On the other hand, a far greater proportion among "fars" than among "nears" have no contact beyond casual greeting and interpret the social climate as unfavorable to contact. The supposition is that a greater proportion of "nears" than "fars" have undergone a change of attitude in a favorable direction and that the contact–social climate experience was instrumental in that change.

It was difficult to assess the relative influence of contact and of the perceived social climate. Among "fars" in both kinds of projects, the influence of each variable on attitude seemed about equal. Among "nears," there was a difference in influence of the two variables depending on the type of project considered: in the integrated projects, contact was the more important variable, in the building-segregated projects, the perceived social climate was the more important. The data of this section also led to an observation of possible theoretical and practical significance—that the perceived social climate seemed to determine attitude even in the absence of contact beyond casual greeting.

An effort was made to suggest a more detailed interpretation of the process of attitude change among white residents of the projects in this study. In these projects the level of contact reached seemed to place a limit on favorableness of attitude. This suggested a stepwise reciprocating interaction of developing contact and changing attitude. The perceived social climate is seen as playing an interlocking role with the contact-attitude process. On the one hand, a social climate perceived as favorable or unfavorable to interracial association facilitates or inhibits the further development of contact in the direction of intimacy, thus promoting or inhibiting the development of further attitude change. On the other hand, the nature of the perceived social climate is seen as shaping attitudes even in the absence of contact.

This account of the process of attitude change is congruent with the data for those living relatively far from Negroes in the project as well as for those living near. Despite earlier emphasis on the difference between "nears" and "fars," it is to be remembered that even among housewives living farther away, about one-third have at least conversational contacts with Negroes and many perceive the social climate as favorable.

CHAPTER VIII

Impact of Occupancy Pattern

THE impact of occupancy pattern on ethnic relations is a question of considerable practical importance since public housing policy is based on the over-all characteristics of a housing project such as integration or segregation and high or low Negro-white ratio.

The Deutsch and Collins study, which focused on comparisons between projects of different occupancy pattern, found marked differences between the integrated projects and the area-segregated projects on all dependent variables; more of the residents of the integrated projects were favorable on every item. It was predicted that in the present study the differences between the integrated and the building-segregated projects would be in the same direction. There were two reasons for this prediction. First, anticipating the general effects of proximity, it seemed clear that at least some white tenants in the integrated projects of the present study lived physically nearer to Negro residents than *any* tenants in the building-segregated projects. Thus, while it was true that some white families in the building-segregated projects lived in buildings adjacent to the all-Negro buildings, a number of white families in the integrated projects lived in the same building with Negroes. Consequently it was expected that in general the integrated projects would give rise to more intimate interracial contact and so would lead to better ethnic relations than in the building-segregated projects.

Secondly, it was expected that the white residents would derive different psychological meanings from the two occupancy patterns. Thus, it was felt that the fact of segregation within the building-segregated projects might be interpreted to mean that the housing authorities themselves were not convinced that interracial mixing was a good idea. This might, in turn, contribute to an over-all social climate unfavorable to contact. The development of widespread contact would have to overcome this psychological barrier. The very fact of integration in the integrated projects would, by contrast, tend to suggest that the

113

authorities assume that racial intermingling is part of the natural order of events.

Several factors, however, led to the expectation that the differences between the two occupancy patterns would be smaller in this study than the differences between occupancy patterns in the Deutsch and Collins study. In the latter study, the combination of a high Negro-white ratio in the integrated projects and the pattern of *area*-segregation in the segregated projects made for considerably greater differences between the two types of projects in the "average" proximity of white to Negro residents. In both integrated projects of the Deutsch and Collins study, almost every white resident lived next door to a Negro resident; in other words, almost all the white residents lived very near Negroes. On the other hand, in the area-segregated projects only the few white residents at the boundary between the Negro and white areas lived even relatively near Negroes; the great majority lived at some distance from Negro residents.

The integrated and segregated projects of the present study do not present such marked contrasts. Because of the small proportion of Negroes, even in the integrated projects relatively few white families live as close to Negroes as did almost all the white families in the Deutsch and Collins integrated projects. On the other hand, the white residents in our building-segregated projects on the average lived closer to Negroes than did those in the Deutsch and Collins area-segregated projects.

It was also expected at the outset of the present study that the differences in psychological meaning between integrated and segregated occupancy patterns would be smaller in this than in the Deutsch and Collins study. In the latter the differences in meaning between the two occupancy patterns must have been especially marked. In the area-segregated projects, the sections were clearly demarcated; not only did white residents live relatively far from Negroes, but they were in a section "for whites only." In the building-segregated projects of the present study, the pattern of segregation was markedly different. Although Negro and white families were housed in separate buildings, the Negro-occupied buildings were interspersed throughout the project. Negro and white tenants used facilities jointly—other than those located within the individual buildings—and there were no functional barriers to interaction between members of the two races. If the fact of segregation within the projects is interpreted as a reservation on the part of the authorities, this reservation is obviously stronger in the case of area-segregated than in the case of building-segregated projects.

It was therefore hypothesized that the differences in extent of contact and attitude would be smaller than those found in the earlier study but in the same direction. In this chapter we shall present data bearing on these hypotheses. As will become apparent later the premises on which the hypotheses were based did not entirely hold; the findings were inconsistent, some comparisons showing the expected differences, some showing no differences. In two instances, the differences were significantly the reverse of our expectations.

Comparison of Integrated and Building-Segregated Projects

Residents of the integrated and the building-segregated projects were compared on all the measures used in assessing the differences between "nears" and "fars" *within* projects. The comparisons between projects of different occupancy pattern were based on representative samples of approximately 150 residents in each project, each sample including all degrees of proximity in the proportion in which they occurred in the given project.

CONTACT BETWEEN THE RACES IN THE PROJECT

As can be seen from Table 40, the differences between projects of the two occupancy patterns are by no means as clear-cut as those between "nears" and "fars" within each of the projects. Between the pair of moderate-rental projects, Integrated I and Building-Segregated I, a significant difference occurs in the proportions of respondents who report engaging in the various kinds of interracial contact. Thus, 34 per cent of those in Integrated I, compared to 15 per cent of those in Building-Segregated I, engage in one or more kinds of neighborly activity. In the pair of low-rental projects, however, little difference appears between Integrated II and Building-Segregated II in the pro-

Table 40. Relation between Occupancy Pattern and the Level of Contact of White Residents with Negro Residents

Level of Contact	Integrated I (150)	Building-Segregated I (172)	Integrated II (150)	Building-Segregated II (135)
No contact	17%	22%	27%	15%
Greets Negroes in casual street encounters	26	33	30	44
Stops to talk in casual street encounters with Negroes ...	23	30	25	27
One or more kinds of neighborly activity	34	15	18	14
χ^2	15.7		10.2	
d.f.	3		3	
p	<.01		<.05	

portions reporting relatively intimate contact with Negroes. Moreover, in this pair of projects, the less-contact end of the scale shows a trend opposed to our prediction: the proportion reporting no contact at all is somewhat greater in the integrated than in the building-segregated project.

EVALUATION OF EXPERIENCES AS PLEASANT OR UNPLEASANT

Table 41 shows the proportions of respondents in each project who reported their experiences with Negroes in the project as exclusively pleasant, as exclusively unpleasant, as mixed, or as neutral. Consistent with the finding concerning proximity groups within projects, these reports correspond rather closely to the reports of level of contact. In every project, more than half the white housewives report that their experiences with Negroes in the project have been neither notably pleasant nor notably unpleasant. Such differences as occur between the integrated and the building-segregated projects are similar to the differences in reports of contact. For example, more of the respondents in Integrated I than in Building-Segregated I reported experiences marked by some kind of feeling tone (43 per cent and 21 per cent, respectively). If we combine "pleasant experiences only" and "mixed pleasant and unpleasant," we find that more respondents in Integrated I than in Building-Segregated I report *some* pleasant experiences with Negroes in the project: 33 per cent and 18 per cent, respectively. In the other pair of projects, Integrated II has a somewhat higher proportion reporting "neither pleasant nor unpleasant experiences." Slightly fewer respondents in Integrated II than in Building-Segregated II report *some* pleasant experiences.

Table 41. Relation between Occupancy Pattern and Evaluation of Experiences with Negroes in the Project as Pleasant or Unpleasant

Evaluation	Integrated I (150)	Building-Segregated I (172)	Integrated II (150)	Building-Segregated II (135)
Pleasant experiences only ..	25%	17%	15%	22%
Pleasant and unpleasant experiences	8	1	5	5
Unpleasant experiences only	10	3	12	15
No pleasant or unpleasant experiences	57	78	68	58
No answer	...	1	...	...
χ^2	21.5		3.7	
d.f.	3		3	
p	<.01		>.10	

ANTICIPATED REACTIONS OF FRIENDS IN THE PROJECT

It might be expected that the differences between integrated and building-segregated projects in anticipated reactions of friends would correspond to the differences in reported level of contact: that in general the differences would be small, that in the case of the moderate-rental projects more respondents in the integrated project would report their friends as favorable, and that in the case of the low-rental projects slightly *fewer* respondents in the integrated project would report their friends as favorable. Table 42 shows, however, that this is not the case. It is true that, as expected, more respondents in Integrated I than in Building-Segregated I report their friends in the project as unqualifiedly favorable to the idea of friendly association with Negroes. Interestingly, the same trend appears in the other pair of projects. Even though the differences in reported contact between Integrated II and Building-Segregated II were minor (if anything, there was *less* contact in the integrated project), respondents in Integrated II are somewhat more likely than those in Building-Segregated II to see their friends as unqualifiedly favorable to the idea of interracial association and considerably less likely to see them as disapproving of such association. In Integrated II, 22 per cent of the white housewives report their friends as unqualifiedly favorable to the idea of friendly association with Negroes, and 41 per cent report their friends as unfavorable; the corresponding figures for Building-Segregated II are 16 per cent favorable, 59 per cent unfavorable.

This tendency for residents of the integrated projects in both pairs to perceive their friends as more favorable to interracial association, even in the absence of differences in actual contact in one of the pairs, suggests that occupancy pattern does influence the perception of social climate even when it does not influence the extent of contact actually occurring between the races.

Table 42. Relation between Occupancy Pattern and Perception of the Social Climate

Anticipated Reaction of White Friends in Project to Friendly Association with Negroes	Integrated I (150)	Building-Segregated I (172)	Integrated II (150)	Building-Segregated II (135)
Unqualifiedly favorable	40%	25%	22%	16%
Mixed or neutral	19	16	20	12
Unfavorable	28	33	41	59
Don't know, not classifiable .	13	26	17	13
χ^2	15.1		10.1	
d.f.	3		3	
p	$<.01$		$<.05$	

INTERPRETING THE INTENTIONS OF MANAGEMENT

Further evidence with respect to the implications of occupancy pattern for perception of social climate may be obtained from the respondents' interpretation of management's intentions regarding interracial association. It will be remembered, from Chapter III, that two aspects were touched on: the attitudes of present management personnel toward friendly association between Negro and white residents, and the presumed reasons for selection by the housing planners of the particular occupancy pattern.

In neither pair of projects is there a significant difference between the integrated and the building-segregated project in the interpretation of the attitudes of present management personnel. Between about three-eighths and about one-half of the respondents in every project perceive management as unqualifiedly favorable to friendly association between Negro and white residents, while less than one-tenth in any project perceive management as completely unfavorable to such association. Evidently few residents in any of the projects find it conceivable that management should wish for anything but racial amity within the project. Under conditions of *building* segregation, where there are no strong functional barriers to contact between white and Negro residents, the fact that they are assigned to separate buildings does not seem to carry the connotation that the present management staff is unfavorable to friendly association between the races.

With respect to the interpretation of the intention of the housing planners in selecting the particular occupancy pattern, however, there were marked differences between the integrated and the segregated projects in both pairs. A different form of the question was used in the two types of projects. In the integrated projects the question was: "Why do you suppose housing planners here arranged for colored and white to live in the same buildings rather than in separate buildings?" The most frequent answer in both projects referred to a desire on the part of the housing planners to effect some sort of social change—"to avoid race prejudice," "feel Negroes are as good as whites," etc. For example, a white respondent in Integrated II commented, "They [the housing planners] think we should all live together to make a better world for all some day," and a respondent in Integrated I felt that the housing planners arranged for integration in order to "stop prejudice; sort of an experiment." Answers of this sort were given by 68 per cent of the respondents in Integrated I and by 54 per cent of the respondents in Integrated II.

In the segregated projects the question was: "Why do you suppose the housing planners have arranged for colored and white to live in separate buildings rather than in the same building?" More than three-quarters of the respondents in each project believed that the housing planners' choice of occupancy pattern derived from feelings or knowledge concerning incompatibility between the races if they lived in the same building—"a lot of fighting if in the same building," "white and colored don't get along together," etc. For example, a white respondent in Building-Segregated II gave the following reason for the segregated pattern of her project: "If a colored person was put next door or too close, the whites would be up in arms, and make it miserable for both manager and colored people." In Building-Segregated I, a white respondent thought the housing planners did not arrange Negroes and whites in the same buildings because "they probably thought white and colored would object strenuously to being that neighborly; it would make for an impossible situation." Answers of this sort were given by 76 per cent of the white respondents in Building-Segregated I and by 87 per cent of those in Building-Segregated II.

It would appear, then, that the motives and reservations of the housing planners (though not of present management personnel) are differently interpreted in the two kinds of projects; it may be that these different interpretations contribute to the differences between the anticipated reactions of friends. However, it must be recognized that the form of the question asked in the building-segregated projects may well have exaggerated the differences. In line with the investigators' classification of these projects as essentially *segregated,* the question contrasted this occupancy pattern with an integrated one. Had the focus been different, the question might have been worded: "Why do you suppose the housing planners arranged for colored and white buildings to be spread out through the project, instead of having them in separate sections?" It seems quite possible that such wording would have elicited answers along lines similar to those given by the respondents in the integrated projects. Our data do not reveal whether the white residents in the building-segregated projects regard them primarily as representing desegregation compared with the community generally, or as representing segregation compared with the possibility of an integrated pattern. The most likely supposition is that both elements are present, and thus that a less structured question with regard to the housing planners' motives would have produced mixed responses. What is clear, however, is that when emphasis is placed on the *segregated* aspect of the occupancy pattern, the great majority of residents draw the inference that the races have been separated because of basic incompatibility between them.

SPECIFIC ATTITUDES

The original hypotheses of the study predicted that residents of the integrated projects would be more favorable than those in the building-segregated projects in various aspects of attitude toward Negroes. Tables 43 and 44, show respectively, the findings for beliefs about characteristics of the Negroes in the project and "esteem" for the Negroes in the project. (Feelings about interracial living, and policy orientation in this respect, will be discussed in the last major section of this chapter.)

Beliefs about Negroes in the project. Table 43 shows the proportions of respondents in each project who believe Negroes and whites are similar in all four characteristics, in two or three of the characteristics, and in only one or none of the characteristics (cleanliness, manners of children, keeping project in good condition, and intelligence). Although slightly more respondents in the integrated than in the building-

Table 43. Relation between Occupancy Pattern and Degree of Belief in the Equality of Negroes and Whites in the Project

Number of Characteristics in Which Races Are Believed Equal	Integrated I (150)	Building-Segregated I (172)	Integrated II (150)	Building-Segregated II (135)
All 4*	40%	33%	29%	18%
2 or 3	37	40	50	57
Only 1 or none	23	27	21	25
χ^2		1.5		4.7
d.f.		2		2
p		>.10		<.10

* As was pointed out in Chapter IV, responses indicating that Negroes were *superior* were grouped with the "equality" responses.

Table 44. Relation between Occupancy Pattern and Degree of "Esteem" for Negroes in the Project

Degree of Esteem	Integrated I (150)	Building-Segregated I (172)	Integrated II (150)	Building-Segregated II (135)
High	50%	61%	43%	47%
Mixed high and low	24	13	30	25
Low	26	21	25	23
Not classifiable	...	5	2	5
χ^2		3.6		0.5
d.f.		2		2
p		>.10		>.10

segregated projects believe that Negroes and whites are similar in all four characteristics, none of the differences is statistically significant. For example, in Integrated II, 29 per cent of the white respondents believed that Negro and white tenants were similar in all four characteristics, compared to 18 per cent in Building-Segregated II, its matched project. However, the two projects were quite similar in the proportions occurring at the other end of the scale: 21 per cent in Integrated II and 25 per cent in Building-Segregated II believed Negro and white tenants were equal in only one or none of the characteristics.

Feelings about Negroes in the project. Table 44 shows the proportions of respondents holding Negroes in the project in various degrees of "esteem." It is apparent that the original hypothesis of more positive feeling in the integrated projects is not supported. Between the two low-rental projects, Integrated II and Building-Segregated II, there were almost no differences at any level of esteem for Negroes in the project. Neither was there a significant difference between the two moderate-rental projects in the distribution of the white respondents throughout *all* the degrees of esteem, although 11 per cent *more* of the white respondents in Building-Segregated I than of those in Integrated I indicated high esteem for Negroes in the project—a finding contrary both to the original hypothesis and to the earlier finding of greater neighborly association in Integrated I.

GENERALIZED ATTITUDES

It will be recalled from Chapter IV that two measures of generalized attitudes were used: a series of five items from the Negro subscale of the California Ethnocentrism Scale and a series of "social distance" items. *Agreement* with the items from the Ethnocentrism Scale signified derogation of Negroes generally. Table 45 shows the proportions of respondents agreeing with various numbers of items on this scale of

Table 45. Relation between Occupancy Pattern and Amount of Agreement with Prejudiced Statements about Negroes in General

Number of Items Agreed with *	Integrated I (150)	Building-Segregated I (172)	Integrated II (150)	Building-Segregated II (135)
At most 1	29%	34%	16%	15%
2 or 3	30	30	23	22
4 or 5	41	36	61	63
χ^2		1.4		.10
d.f.		2		2
p		>.10		>.10

* Agreement indicates a negative attitude toward Negroes.

generalized attitude toward Negroes; agreement with at most one item represents the *least* prejudiced attitude, agreement with four or five items the *most* prejudiced. Here again, there is little difference between the two projects of each pair on this scale of generalized attitudes. The distributions in the two low-rental projects are almost identical. In the moderate-rental pair, such slight differences as do occur are in favor of the building-segregated project.

On the social-distance scale, the only differences between integrated and segregated projects occurred on the item with respect to having Negroes as tenants in the same building. This point will be discussed in detail in the following section.

ATTITUDES WITH RESPECT TO INTERRACIAL LIVING

It will be recalled from Chapter IV that respondents were asked a series of questions intended to tap their *feelings* about living in a mixed Negro-white project and their *policy orientation* regarding the arrangement of Negro and white dwelling units in future public housing projects.

Feelings about biracial character of project. Table 46 shows the responses to the questions pertaining to the white respondents' feelings about living in a Negro-white project. In both pairs of projects there are substantial differences in the direction opposite to that predicted by the original hypothesis; that is, in both cases respondents in the integrated projects are more likely to *disapprove* of the biracial character of the project than are those in the building-segregated projects. In the moderate-rental projects, 45 per cent of the white respondents in Integrated I expressed dislike of living in a biracial project, compared to 23 per cent in Building-Segregated I. The difference between Integrated II and Building-Segregated II is not quite so marked, but is still greater than would be likely to occur by chance; 57 per cent of white respondents in Integrated II, as compared with 44 per cent in

Table 46. Relation between Occupancy Pattern and Feelings about Living in a Negro-White Project

Feeling	Integrated I (150)	Building-Segregated I (172)	Integrated II (150)	Building-Segregated II (135)
Approval	27%	38%	24%	24%
Mixed	27	33	18	26
Disapproval	45	23	57	44
Not classifiable	1	6	1	6
χ^2		18.0		9.5
d.f.		3		3
p		<.01		<.05

Building-Segregated II, expressed disapproval of the biracial character of their project.

It will be recalled that respondents were asked specifically what things they liked and what things they did not like about living in a biracial project. The most frequent categories of favorable response were the following: pleasant traits and actions of Negroes in the project, ideological factors related to the democratic ideal of equality, and helping children avoid prejudice. In the first of these categories, pleasant traits and actions of Negroes, there was no difference between the integrated and the building-segregated projects in either pair; about a quarter of the white respondents in each of the projects mentioned this particular pleasant aspect. In the second category, ideological factors, there was no difference between Integrated I and Building-Segregated I. In the other pair of projects, however, there was a difference in the proportions of respondents mentioning this factor; a greater proportion in Building-Segregated II (38 per cent) than in Integrated II (27 per cent) mentioned it. The third category, helping children to avoid prejudice, was, in both pairs of projects, mentioned more frequently by residents of the building-segregated projects.

A corresponding difference between the proportions who expressed approval of letting Negro and white children play together was found in the moderate-rental projects; 83 per cent of the respondents in Building-Segregated I, compared to 66 per cent in Integrated I, said they approved. There was no difference between the projects of the other pair; about one-half of the white respondents in each project expressed approval.

In short, any differences found with respect to feelings about various aspects of living in an interracial project were in the direction opposite to that which had been predicted; respondents in the building-segregated projects were *more* likely to be favorable than were those in the integrated projects.

Policy orientation with respect to occupancy pattern. It will be recalled that the question asking for recommendations as to occupancy pattern to be followed in future projects presented three alternatives: that Negroes and whites should live "anywhere in the project," "in separate buildings," or "in separate projects." Table 47 shows the proportion in each project recommending each of these patterns.

A greater proportion of respondents in the integrated than in the building-segregated projects choose the alternative of completely separate projects; the proportions are 44 per cent in Integrated I to 26 per cent in Building-Segregated I, and 67 per cent in Integrated II to 55 per cent in Building-Segregated II. And since recommendations of

Table 47. Relation between Occupancy Pattern and Recommendation for
Future Projects

Recommended Pattern for Negroes and Whites	Integrated I (150)	Building-Segregated I (172)	Integrated II (150)	Building-Segregated II (135)
Live anywhere in the project	34%	13%	17%	1%
Live in separate buildings	21	60	14	44
Live in separate projects	44	26	67	55
Don't know, no answer	1	1	2	...
χ^2	49.9		45.7	
d.f. (end categories combined)	2		2	
p	<.01		<.01	

separate projects is the "least favorable" response, this result is opposite to the direction predicted by the hypotheses. In both pairs of
projects, a far greater proportion of respondents in the building-segregated than in the integrated projects recommend the pattern which
the former have themselves experienced—that of assigning Negroes
and whites to separate buildings within the same project. The one
finding in line with the hypotheses is that in each pair of projects a
greater proportion of respondents in the integrated than in the segregated project recommend that Negroes and whites live anywhere in the
project, that is, recommend an integrated occupancy pattern. The proportions are 34 per cent in Integrated I to 13 per cent in Building-
Segregated I, and 17 per cent in Integrated II to 1 per cent in Building-
Segregated II. Since recommendations of integrated occupancy pattern
is the "most favorable" response, this finding supports the hypotheses.

It will be noted, comparing Tables 46 and 47, that the proportions
in each project recommending separate projects for the future resemble quite closely the proportions in each project expressing disapproval of the fact that they are themselves living in a mixed project.
This suggests that dissatisfaction with present "mixed" arrangements
—whether integrated or building-segregated—is associated with rejection of the whole idea of biracial living.

Table 48, which shows for each project the occupancy pattern recommendations of those who approve and disapprove of the fact that they
are now living in a biracial project, reveals that this relationship is
very high. In every project no fewer than two-thirds of those expressing unqualified disapproval recommend separate projects; almost no
one among these respondents recommends integration.

For those who approve of living in a biracial project, the picture is
different. In every project, the great majority of these respondents

Table 48. Relation between Occupancy Pattern Recommended for Future Projects and Present Attitude of Tenants toward Living in a Negro-White Project *

Recommended Pattern for Negroes and Whites	Integrated I		Building-Segregated I		Integrated II		Building-Segregated II	
	Approval (40)	Disapproval (67)	Approval (66)	Disapproval (41)	Approval (36)	Disapproval (86)	Approval (33)	Disapproval (60)
Live anywhere in the project	68%	6%	24%	...	53%	5%	...	...
Live in separate buildings	17	22	66	34%	19	8	76%	22%
Live in separate projects	15	70	8	66	28	86	24	78
Don't know, no answer	...	2	2	...	...	1	...	...

* Respondents who gave answers signifying mixed approval and disapproval on this item have been omitted.

(seven-tenths or more) recommend some arrangement whereby Negroes and whites are housed in the same project. But, in every project, more than half of those who approve of biracial living recommend the *same* occupancy pattern for future projects as exists in the one they inhabit. In the two building-segregated projects, at least two-thirds of the respondents who themselves like living in a mixed project recommend building-segregation as the pattern for future projects. Of the remainder, all in Building-Segregated II recommend separate projects, whereas most in Building-Segregated I, recommend "anywhere in the project." In the two integrated projects, more than half of the respondents who themselves like living in a mixed project recommend *integration* as the pattern for future projects; the remainder recommend separate buildings and separate projects about equally.

When we consider the data on attitudes toward occupancy pattern in view of the data on beliefs about and feelings toward Negroes, it would appear that living in a building-segregated project permits quite favorable attitudes from the standpoint of feelings and beliefs but that these favorable attitudes are not extended to include policy orientation. On the other hand, living in an integrated project, while not having any advantage over the building-segregated projects in engendering favorable feelings and beliefs, does permit an extension of the latter into policy orientation. Thus, considering the project pairs, while the differences on the belief and feeling items with respect to Negroes is relatively small, there are considerably higher proportions favoring integrated housing in the integrated than in the building-segregated projects. This is not to gainsay that even in the integrated projects there were substantially higher proportions in favor of complete segregation than in favor of integration. This might indicate that a great many were not being consistent with their expressed beliefs and feelings, but it also might indicate that there were comparatively many more in the integrated than in the building-segregated projects who apparently were being consistent.

In the building-segregated projects, rejection of an integrated occupancy pattern seems supported by the respondents' interpretations of the motives of the project-builders in establishing the pattern of building-segregation. It will be recalled that at least three-quarters of the respondents in the building-segregated projects, regardless of proximity to Negroes, felt that a major reason for assigning Negroes and whites to separate buildings was the fear that the races would not get along if they were in the same building. When asked to account for their own recommendations for future projects, respondents again referred to this belief; even those who themselves had unstereotyped beliefs about the Negroes in the project and high "esteem" for them were likely to echo the fears about racial incompatibility which they had attributed to management. There was frequent mention of possible prejudiced behavior on the part of certain whites (southerners, for instance), and of feelings of discomfort or "strangeness" over living in the same building; some respondents said outright that while they liked the Negroes in the project, it was nice to be able to go back to their own building.

In the integrated projects, on the other hand, while not everyone who held relatively unstereotyped beliefs about Negroes and who held them in high "esteem" recommended the integrated occupancy pattern, a fairly large proportion did. In this case acceptance of Negroes was in the context of living in a project with same-building tenancy.* There was furthermore little possibility of interpreting management's intentions as supporting some sort of separation between the races. On the contrary, at least half the respondents in the integrated projects interpreted the intention underlying the project pattern as promoting good ethnic relations.

The over-all principle, then, on which Negroes and whites are arranged in the projects has some bearing on policy orientation, a socially important dimension of intergroup attitude. White persons living near Negroes in a building-segregated project may have considerable contact with them, may, as we have shown, undergo favorable change in

---

*It is worth noting that while in the integrated projects there were the expected "near"-"far" differences in recommendations of future occupancy pattern, even the "fars" (who lived in all-white buildings) in these projects were more likely than *any* respondents in the matched building-segregated projects to recommend integration.

beliefs and feelings about Negroes, and may now be more favorable to biracial living. But the clearly visible principle of apartment assignment to separate buildings, accompanied by the widespread interpretation that otherwise there would be "trouble," seems to inhibit strongly the willingness to admit Negroes to the closest residential arrangement.*

Summary

We have compared the two integrated projects with their matched building-segregated projects on the dependent variables of the study. The basic hypothesis was that the proportion of respondents having more than superficial contact, perceiving the social climate regarding interracial association as favorable, and holding favorable attitudes in all dimensions would be greater in the integrated than in the matched building-segregated projects.

The results are inconsistent: on some items the hypothesis was confirmed, on others the differences between projects were slight, and on two items there was a marked reversal. With regard to extent of interracial contact, the hypothesis was confirmed only in the moderate-rental projects, a significantly greater proportion in the integrated than in the building-segregated project reporting contact with Negroes. With regard to perception of the informal pressures encouraging or discouraging contacts, the hypothesis was confirmed in both sets of projects. In each case a significantly greater proportion in the integrated projects than in their building-segregated matches anticipated favorable reactions from their friends in the project in the event of their friendly association with Negroes. On the other hand, on "beliefs," "esteem," and "generalization," the differences between projects, sometimes in the expected direction and sometimes in the reverse, were not statistically significant.

Regarding satisfaction with living in the projects, there was a consistent reversal; in each matched pair, a greater proportion in the integrated projects expressed disapproval of living in a Negro-white project. With respect to "policy orientation," the relationship was complex: while a greater proportion in the integrated than in the building-segregated projects recommended completely separate arrangements in future projects (opposite to the hypothesis), a greater proportion in

---

* The tendency to approve of the type of occupancy pattern with which one has experience is confirmed in the Deutsch and Collins study. In that study about half the respondents in the integrated projects recommended integration, while practically none of those in the area-segregated projects did so. Living in area segregation made even building segregation a relatively extreme suggestion: only one-quarter recommended it, while almost three-quarters favored separate projects, the occupancy type closest to their own experience.

the integrated projects also recommended an integrated occupancy pattern (supporting the hypothesis). Respondents in the building-segregated projects were the most likely to recommend a separate building arrangement, and very few recommended integration.

In all projects the white residents' expressed disapproval of living in a biracial project was highly associated with recommendations for completely separate projects. On the other hand, approval of living in a biracial project resulted in different recommendations: in each integrated project, a majority recommended integration; in each building-segregated project a majority recommended building-segregation.

CHAPTER IX

Factors Obscuring the Effects
of Occupancy Pattern

THE expectation of differences in contact and attitude between the residents of the projects of the two occupancy-pattern types is based on the same premises as the expectation of such differences between those living "near" and those living "far" from Negroes. Yet in the latter case our hypotheses are strikingly confirmed whereas in the former they are not. How is this to be explained?

Reconsideration of the logical development of the hypotheses points up the fact that there is one premise which plays a role in determining the occupancy-pattern expectations which does not enter into the "near"-"far" expectations. This is the assumption that there are systematic differences in proximity which are related to occupancy pattern. On the face of it, this seemed like a reasonable assumption. Obviously, if there are white residents in the integrated projects living in the same building as Negroes there must be at least some whites who live closer to Negroes than do white residents in the building-segregated projects where no whites live in the same buildings with Negroes. It seemed reasonable to assume that this would make for a systematic difference between the two sets of projects. Nevertheless, the inconsistency in our findings—i.e., confirmation of the hypotheses in the case of the "near"-"far" analysis and considerably less confirmation in the case of the occupancy-pattern analysis—makes it necessary to re-examine this assumption. It is conceivable that the over-all distribution of Negro families is such that there is little difference in the average proximities of the total tenant bodies. This possibility becomes all the more plausible when we consider the fact that the proportion of Negroes in our projects is only 10 per cent. It becomes necessary, therefore, to examine the average proximities in the two types of projects.

"Average" Proximity of White to Negro Residents

Let us consider first the matched moderate-rental projects. In Integrated I, Negro tenants are evenly dispersed in apartments throughout the project; in general, one Negro family is found in a cluster of four or five buildings. In all, 29 per cent of the white residents live in buildings where there is a Negro tenant; the remainder live in all-white buildings. In Building-Segregated I, to be sure, 56 per cent of the white residents live in all-white courts, and so may be thought of as farther from Negroes than are most of the white residents of Integrated I. However, the remainder, 44 per cent, live in mixed courts.

Another factor must also be taken into account. In Integrated I as a consequence of the low Negro-white ratio (one Negro family to a cluster of buildings), the white residents' opportunities for contact with Negroes are limited not only by their degree of proximity but by factors—involving both statistical probabilities and considerations of congeniality, common interests, etc.—which limit the likelihood of contact with that particular Negro family. On the other hand, those residents of Building-Segregated I who live in mixed courts find themselves in a situation where there are several Negro families, constituting at least 25 per cent of the population in the immediate vicinity. The interviews revealed that in Building-Segregated I, 98 per cent of those living in mixed courts who knew Negroes in the project knew *several* well enough to be able to specify where they lived, while in Integrated I, among those who lived in mixed buildings and knew Negroes in the project, only 64 per cent knew the home location of more than one Negro family. The opportunities for interracial contact may hence be greater for the white residents of these mixed courts in Building-Segregated I than for most of the white residents of Integrated I.

A very similar analysis may be made of the matched low-rental projects. In Integrated II, 42 per cent live in all-white buildings in an area where the proportion of Negroes to whites is less than one in twenty, and another 14 per cent live in a completely all-white area. (The relatively high proportion of respondents in this project reporting no contact whatsoever with Negroes arises largely from these latter groups.) For the project as a whole, then, the nearness of whites to Negroes in the mixed buildings may be offset by the large proportion who live at relatively great distance from Negroes. In Building-Segregated II, on the other hand, while it is true that the white residents live in all-white buildings, only 22 per cent live in areas relatively isolated from Negro buildings, and 19 per cent live in buildings immediately adjacent to a building occupied by Negro residents.

The second factor must be taken into account in this instance also.

Of the white families in Integrated II who live in *mixed buildings*, more than half (59 per cent) are in buildings that contain only a single Negro family, in areas where the proportion of Negroes is less than 5 per cent of the total area population. In other words, for more than half even of those white housewives who live in mixed buildings, there is only a single Negro family in the effective vicinity with whom contacts may reasonably be expected to occur. In Building-Segregated II, on the other hand, those who live next to a Negro-occupied building, or even in the general neighborhood of such a building, have opportunity for contact with from six to eight Negro families.

It seems clear that the differences in average proximity of white to Negro residents which we had assumed would hold for the two types of biracial project do not, in fact, obtain. The failure of this assumption explains the inconsistency between our own two sets of findings, and also the difference between our findings and those reported by Deutsch and Collins with respect to occupancy pattern. Not only is it true, as we have already explained earlier, that the differences in "average proximity" between the integrated and the building-segregated projects of the present study were considerably less than the differences in "average proximity" between the integrated and the area-segregated projects of the Deutsch and Collins study, but it is also the case that the proportion of Negroes was very much higher in the Deutsch and Collins study, ranging from 40 to 70 per cent compared to our 10 per cent. The effect of the latter difference between the settings of the two studies is that a white resident in the Deutsch and Collins integrated projects would find it more difficult *not* to experience at least superficial contact with Negroes than would a white resident in our integrated projects.

Moreover, with respect to the functional or psychological barriers introduced by a segregated occupancy pattern, it has been pointed out (in the discussion in Chapter II, comparing the present study with that of Deutsch and Collins) that such barriers in a building-segregated project are quite different from those in an area-segregated project. In a building-segregated project, white and Negro tenants share the same walks, the same laundry facilities, the same parking areas. It seems possible that the pattern of building segregation may introduce barriers only against the most intimate level of contact, the home-centered neighborly activities. As a matter of fact, in one of the matched pairs of projects (Integrated I and Building-Segregated I) differences reflecting this possible barrier do appear at this level of contact.

Comparability of Factors Other than Occupancy Pattern

It would thus appear that the failure to confirm our predictions with respect to the two types of occupancy pattern does not contradict the underlying hypothesis—already confirmed in the "near"-"far" analysis —that in general proximity leads to contact, which leads to attitude change, which leads to more intimate contact, which leads to more attitude change, and so on, until some undetermined limit is reached. From the viewpoint of practical application in public housing policies, it is, of course, worth knowing that an integrated pattern does not automatically make for as great proximity as one might expect and that a building-segregated pattern does not necessarily make for as little proximity as one might expect. This is because other factors enter into proximity—for instance, the ratio of Negro to white residents and the type of architecture, i.e., whether the buildings are set around a common court or arranged in a straight line.

It seems desirable, however, to examine whether there are not factors other than the lack of difference in proximity that might be obscuring the differences between our two occupancy pattern types. If such factors were found, differences between occupancy patterns might then appear even under our proximity conditions. Thus such factors might account for the instances of the reversal of our expectation. At least two such possibilities suggest themselves. One of these has to do with differences in specific situational factors that might operate in a direction opposite to our expectations. The second is that although there were no significant differences in the estimated initial comparability of the "nears" and the "fars" within any project, there might nevertheless have been over-all differences in initial comparability of white tenants between the two types of project. We now turn, therefore, to an examination of each of these two possibilities, first for the low-rental projects and then for the two moderate-rental projects.

MATCHED LOW-RENTAL PROJECTS

Situational factors. Let us examine briefly certain situational factors apart from occupancy patterns which may have tended to promote or inhibit interracial contact and thus more favorable attitudes in one and not the other project. While the two low-rental projects were quite similar in building type, rent, income limitations, etc., there were, nevertheless, certain differences which may have influenced the course of ethnic relations.

First, the management staff in Integrated II was all white, while Building-Segregated II had an interracial managerial staff, the manager being white and his assistant Negro. This assistant, a woman, ordinarily had more contact with the tenants than did the manager himself, who was frequently away from the office because of other duties.

The presence of a Negro in a responsible position on the staff may have played an important role in establishing the level of interaction between the races.*

Second, in Integrated II there had been a change in policy with respect to occupancy pattern about three years before the present study. Before that time Negroes had, for the most part, been placed only in one fairly large section of the project, although in that section they were in buildings with white tenants. After the change in policy, Negroes were assigned apartments throughout the project, although there were still some sections with few or no Negro families. The originally inconsistent policy or the shift in policy may have brought various tensions, the effects of which might still be felt. In Building-Segregated II, on the other hand, the occupancy pattern had remained unchanged since the project was first occupied.

Third, in the city where Integrated II is located, there are a number of all-white and all-Negro projects as well as several which are integrated. In the city where Building-Segregated II is located, building segregation has been the established policy in all projects since the inauguration of the first public housing project there; moreover, the city has been considered a pioneer in the establishment of biracial housing.

It is difficult to assess the impact of these situational differences accurately. Nevertheless, it seems possible that all of the factors mentioned (the presence of an interracial management staff in Building-Segregated II but not in Integrated II, the change in apartment assignment policy within Integrated II, and the greater city-wide consistency of Housing Authority policy in the community where Building-Segregated II is located) might have operated to increase the greater probability of interracial contacts and of favorable attitudes in Building-Segregated II than in Integrated II.

Initial comparability of attitudes. While some of the known or supposed correlates of initial attitude show little difference between respondents in the two projects, there are a number which show substantial differences in a direction which would work against our hypotheses. There are, for example, in Integrated II, as compared with Building-Segregated II, a greater proportion of residents who voted Republican (42 per cent to 22 per cent); a greater proportion with less than eighth-grade education (30 per cent to 18 per cent); a greater proportion reporting initially unfavorable impressions of Negroes (51 per cent to 35 per cent); a greater proportion reporting that none of

* Compare the review of the experience of housing officials on this point in Deutsch and Collins (7), pp. 13–14.

their friends or relatives approve of their living in a Negro-white project "like this one" (33 per cent to 22 per cent); and fewer reporting incomes over $50 a week (23 per cent to 60 per cent). All of these differences suggest the likelihood that the white residents of Integrated II were initially less favorably disposed to Negroes than were those in Building-Segregated II.

The differences between projects may be summarized by constructing an index of estimated initial attitude made up of the five items that showed the closest relation to ethnic attitude within each of the low-rental projects: income, original impression of Negroes, political party preference, education, and prior knowledge of Negroes' presence in the project.

Table 49. Distribution of Tenants on an Index of Estimated Initial Attitude toward Negroes, by Occupancy Pattern in the Low-Rental Projects

Number of Items Indicating Probable Pro-Negro Position*	Integrated II (150)	Building-Segregated II (135)
4 or 5	5%	18%
2 or 3	61	65
0 or 1	34	17

*The items that enter into the index for this comparison are income, reported prior impression of Negroes, political party preference, education, and prior knowledge of the presence of Negroes in the project.

Table 49 compares the respondents in the two projects on this index. It supports the assumption that a greater proportion of the respondents in Building-Segregated II than of those in Integrated II were initially more favorable in attitudes toward Negroes. Eighteen per cent of the respondents in Building-Segregated II, compared to only 5 per cent of those in Integrated II, are in the position believed most likely to indicate relatively favorable attitude toward Negroes; at the other end of the scale, 17 per cent in Building-Segregated II and 34 per cent in Integrated II are in the position believed most likely to indicate unfavorable initial attitude.

Whether this difference is in a sense an accidental one, having to do with, say, the location of the projects within their respective cities, or whether it reflects systematic differences in "city atmosphere" of which we are not aware, is difficult to say. In any case, it seems fairly clear that there were substantial differences in estimated initial attitude which would operate in the direction opposite to our original hypotheses, that is, which would tend to result in more contact and more favorable attitudes in the building-segregated project.

It is possible, however, to compensate for the impact of this differential distribution of initial attitude. This was done by equating subsamples in both projects so that they contained a similar distribution of positions on the index of initial attitude. Excess cases on each index level were randomly eliminated. For example, as shown in Table 49, 34 per cent of the respondents in Integrated II fell in the category indicating a probable pro-Negro position on at most one item ("0 or 1") as compared with 17 per cent of those in Building-Segregated II. In order to eliminate the overweighting of Integrated II on this category, it was necessary to remove excess cases. Also, the number of cases in Building-Segregated II in the category indicating a probable pro-Negro position on at least four items ("4 or 5") had to be reduced. This process of matching left us with two subsamples (119 cases in Integrated II and 107 cases in Building-Segregated II) with similar proportions of cases at each position on the index. The proportions of these new samples having various degrees of contact with Negroes, various degrees of "esteem" for them, etc., were then recalculated.

Comparisons based on the "matched" samples are shown in Tables 50 to 55 and reveal considerable changes in results on all the major dependent variables. All of these changes are in the direction of greater accord with the original hypotheses, although on most of the variables the differences between projects are still not statistically significant. Thus, the small reverse trends in extent of contact and "esteem" which occurred in the uncorrected samples now disappear, as do the more substantial originally reverse findings with regard to feelings about living in a mixed project.

MATCHED MODERATE-RENTAL PROJECTS

Situational factors. The two moderate-rental projects were similar on a number of characteristics: both were relatively new, had similar building type, etc. There were, however, certain differences between the projects, other than occupancy pattern, which might have influenced the course of interracial relations.

First, at the time of the interviewing, Building-Segregated I had a sporadically functioning tenants' organization, which included Negroes among its active members; Integrated I had no tenants' organization.

Second, although the building type was much the same in the two projects, the arrangement of the buildings was different. In Building-Segregated I, all the buildings were arranged in courts, with four or five buildings to a court, whereas in Integrated I the buildings were grouped in straight-line clusters, with only an occasional courtlike arrangement. The arrangement of buildings in clearly marked out

Table 50. Distribution of Tenants on the Basis of Level of Contact, by
Occupancy Pattern in the Low-Rental Projects, Subsamples Being
Equated for Estimated Initial Attitude

Level of Contact with Negroes in Project	Integrated II (119)	Building- Segregated II (107)
No contact	24%	16%
Greets Negroes in casual street encounters	30	47
Stops to talk in casual street encounters with Negroes	28	25
One or more kinds of neighborly activity	18	12

Table 51. Distribution of Tenants on the Basis of Perception of the Social
Climate, by Occupancy Pattern in the Low-Rental Projects,
Subsamples Being Equated for Estimated Initial Attitude

Anticipated Reaction of White Friends in Project to Friendly Association with Negroes	Integrated II (119)	Building- Segregated II (107)
Unqualifiedly favorable	42%	22%
Mixed or neutral	4	4
Unfavorable	36	62
Don't know, not classifiable	18	12

Table 52. Distribution of Tenants on the Basis of "Esteem" for Negroes
in the Project, by Occupancy Pattern in the Low-Rental Projects,
Subsamples Being Equated for Estimated Initial Attitude

Degree of Esteem	Integrated II (119)	Building- Segregated II (107)
High	48%	41%
Mixed high and low	24	24
Low	25	29
Not classifiable	3	6

Table 53. Distribution of Tenants on the Basis of the Amount of Agree-
ment with Prejudiced Statements about Negroes in General, by
Occupancy Pattern in the Low-Rental Projects, Subsamples Being
Equated for Estimated Initial Attitude

Number of Items Agreed with *	Integrated II (119)	Building- Segregated II (107)
At most 1	17%	12%
2 or 3	26	18
4 or 5	57	70

* Agreement indicates a negative attitude toward Negroes.

Table 54. Distribution of Tenants on the Basis of Feelings about Living in a Negro-White Project, by Occupancy Pattern in the Low-Rental Projects, Subsamples Being Equated for Estimated Initial Attitude

Feeling	Integrated II (119)	Building-Segregated II (107)
Approval	28%	21%
Mixed	19	24
Disapproval	52	48
Not classifiable	1	7

Table 55. Distribution of Tenants on the Basis of the Pattern They Recommend for Future Projects, by Occupancy Pattern in the Low-Rental Projects, Subsamples Being Equated for Estimated Initial Attitude

Recommended Pattern for Negroes and Whites	Integrated II (119)	Building-Segregated II (107)
Live anywhere in the project	19%	...
Live in separate buildings	13	40%
Live in separate projects	68	60
Don't know, no answer	...	...

courts offers the possibility of more association between tenants in the different buildings than does a straight-line arrangement, since the court setup makes for greater common use of such facilities as walks and yards.

Third, factors having to do more with general community atmosphere than with conditions within the projects themselves must be taken into account. One factor of this sort is the clarity of the policy of the Housing Authority in the respective projects with regard to occupancy pattern. In the city where Building-Segregated I is located, building segregation was the long-established policy, uniform in all projects throughout the city. On the other hand, in the city where Integrated I is located, there was no such consistent policy. Integrated I was the *first* integrated project in the city and, even at the time of the study, there were in this community all-white and all-Negro projects as well as several integrated ones. Moreover, a member of the Housing Authority had publicly stated that one of the most desirable projects was to be reserved for white occupancy. The effect of these differences in consistency of Housing Authority policy on the attitude of white tenants was not determined; as a matter of fact, we do not even know to what extent tenants were aware of the consistency or inconsistency of policy. It seems possible, however, that at least overtones of these policies might have been conveyed in some way to the tenants and might have helped to set the social atmosphere with regard to interracial living.

Another factor having to do with general community atmosphere was that for a period of five years before the present study, the community in which Building-Segregated I is located had had a city-wide campaign against prejudice, launched by a mayor's committee and carried out with the cooperation of many of the city's residents. The precise influence of such a campaign is, of course, difficult to determine, but it should be noted that another study conducted on a city-wide basis shortly before interviewing for the present study was begun in Building-Segregated I revealed that those white residents of the city who had been exposed to the campaign were more likely to show favorable attitudes toward Negroes than were white residents without such exposure. In the present study, 31 per cent of the white residents in Building-Segregated I knew something of the antiprejudice campaign (and, consistent with the other study just cited, held more favorable attitudes toward Negroes than those who knew nothing about the campaign). There was no such program in the city in which Integrated I is located. The existence of this campaign and its rather long duration before the time of the present study suggest that the residents of Building-Segregated I, although similar to those of Integrated I on the index of estimated initial attitude (as will be shown in the section immediately following) may nevertheless have been initially less prejudiced in aspects not covered by this index. Less prejudice may have been attributable to a favorable community atmosphere, and the effects of the white residents' experience of living in a biracial project may have been reinforced by this more favorable atmosphere in the surrounding community.

While the influence of the tenants' organization, the project layout, and the community "atmosphere" is difficult to specify, it is conceivable that all these factors operated to increase the probability of interracial contacts in Building-Segregated I as compared to Integrated I, or to decrease the probability of such contact in the integrated as compared to the segregated project.

Initial comparability of attitudes. Some of the known or supposed correlates of initial attitude toward Negroes show little difference between the respondents in Integrated I and those in Building-Segregated I. However, there are a number which show substantial differences in a direction which would work against our original hypotheses; that is, on a number of items it would appear that respondents in Building-Segregated I were likely to have been initially more favorably disposed than those in Integrated I.

There are, for instance, in Integrated I, compared with Building-Segregated I, a greater proportion who had a "predominantly nega-tive" initial impression of Negroes (51 per cent to 37 per cent), a great-er proportion reporting that none of their friends or relatives approve of their living in a Negro-white project "like this one" (31 per cent to 10 per cent), and a greater proportion who have had no prior contact with Negroes (41 per cent to 29 per cent). A summary of these differ-ences was obtained by constructing an index of estimated initial atti-tude made up of the five items that showed the closest relation to ethnic attitude within each of the moderate-rental projects: income, reported prior impression of Negroes, previous contact with Negroes, religion, and prior knowledge of Negroes' presence in the project.

Table 56. Distribution of Tenants on an Index of Estimated Initial Attitude toward Negroes, by Occupancy Pattern in the Moderate-Rental Projects

Number of Items Indicating Probable Pro-Negro Position *	Integrated I (150)	Building-Segregated I (172)
4 or 5	15%	17%
2 or 3	54	60
0 or 1	31	23

* The items that enter into the index for this comparison are income, reported prior impression of Negroes, previous contact with Negroes, reli-gion, and prior knowledge of the presence of Negroes in the project.

Table 56 compares the respondents in the two projects on this index. While there seems to be a slight tendency for residents in Building-Segregated I to have been more favorably predisposed toward Negroes than were those in Integrated I, the difference is one which might easily have occurred by chance. In other words, when we combine those items which seem to distinguish most sharply between the two projects, the result does not bear out the suggestion based on a number of individual items that respondents in Building-Segregated I were more favorably predisposed toward Negroes than were respondents in Integrated I. We may conclude that such differences in the dependent variables as occur between projects may be attributed only in very small part, if at all, to differences in personal characteristics between the residents in the two projects which predisposed them to more or less favorable atti-tudes toward Negroes.

As might be expected from the slight differences on the index of esti-mated initial attitude, comparisons based on the "matched" sub-samples in the two projects showed essentially the same results as those based on the representative project samples; at most there were changes of two or three percentage points in the direction of congruence with the basic hypotheses. For example, the uncorrected project samples showed 11 per cent more in Building-Segregated I than in Integrated I holding Negroes in the project in high esteem; after adjustment for initial comparability, the difference is 8 per cent. Similar insignificant changes appear on the other variables; on none is there any essential change in the positions of the two projects.

For the moderate-rental projects, then, the picture remains the same whether we use total project sample or equated subsamples in the comparisons: the findings are compatible with the hypothesis on several items; there is no relationship between occupancy patterns and attitude on several others; and there is a reversal of expectation on the item concerning satisfaction with living in a Negro-white project.

Summary

The pairs of projects of the present study, matched by type of occupancy pattern, showed differences in the dependent variables of the present study which were, in general, small and not consistently in favor of one or the other pattern. The results of the earlier "near"-"far" analysis—so strikingly in conformity with our hypotheses—suggested that our premise was incorrect regarding a relationship between systematic differences in proximity and occupancy pattern. This suspicion was supported by an examination of the evidence bearing on the question of proximity. Differences in the "average" proximity of white to Negro residents between the matched projects are probably quite small, certainly smaller than between the Deutsch and Collins matched projects.

Since occupancy pattern is a concept of considerable practical importance for social policy, it seemed desirable to determine whether there might not be factors other than proximity which were operative and which, through having an independent influence on the behavior and attitudes of white residents in each type of project, would obscure our results. In an examination of the influence of certain situational factors, it appeared in each matched pair of projects that a number of conditions existed which may have counteracted the original hypotheses. We infer with some degree of confidence that the absence of these differential conditions which are unrelated to occupancy pattern and, in a sense, occur accidentally, would quite likely have favored the original hypotheses about the impact of occupancy pattern.[*]

[*] For obvious reasons our focus in this chapter has been on the situational and initial attitude comparisons of matched projects that differed in occupancy pattern. Clearly, projects of the same occupancy pattern may differ in situational factors and the respondents may differ in initial attitude. In the present study, the more favorable attitudes occurring in Integrated I than in Integrated II and in Building-Segregated I than in Building-Segregated II might be accounted for in this way.

The same line of reasoning indicated the desirability of inquiring whether the respondents in each project of the matched pairs were initially comparable in ethnic attitude at the time of moving in. It might have been, for example, that the hypothesized favorable influence of the integrated projects was obscured by the accidental (for the study) occurrence of less favorable initial attitudes among respondents in the integrated projects. An index of estimated initial attitude constructed from several items known to be correlated with ethnic attitude showed that this was indeed the case in the low-rental projects. There were marked differences between the matched low-rental projects. In the moderate-rental projects there were smaller differences between matched projects. In both cases residents of the integrated projects were initially *less* favorably disposed than those in the comparable building-segregated projects.

When the samples of respondents in each set of matched projects were equated for initial attitude, the results moved in a direction congruent with the basic hypothesis. In the low-rental projects the movement was considerable. There were now no reversals of the expected relationships, although the differences between projects were smaller than in the Deutsch and Collins study. In the moderate-rental projects, as might be expected from the lesser initial differences, the adjustment of the samples had a smaller effect. While there was clearly evidence of more interracial contact and a more favorable informal social climate regarding this contact in the integrated project, attitude differences were still slight and, in one case, opposite to expectation to a statistically significant degree. On the matter of satisfaction with living in a biracial project, there remained a greater proportion in the integrated project who expressed disapproval. On recommendations for the future the original complex finding was essentially unaltered. We may assume that in this pair of projects the situational factors played a much more important role than did initial comparability.

Thus, in general, while our hypotheses regarding the influence of occupancy pattern have not been entirely confirmed, they have also not been contradicted by the findings reported in the preceding chapter.

CHAPTER X

Comparison of Results
with the Deutsch and Collins Findings

On all the dependent variables considered—level of contact, perception of social climate, and various attitude components—both the integrated and the building-segregated projects of the present study fell between the extremes found in the integrated and the area-segregated projects of the Deutsch and Collins study. This was expected, since the small proportion of Negroes in the present projects resulted in fewer white residents in the integrated projects living next door to Negroes and since, both functionally and in terms of physical distance, the separation between Negroes and whites in the present building-segregated projects was less sharp than in the Deutsch and Collins area-segregated projects. In other words, the "average" proximity in all four projects of the present study lay somewhere between the extremes of the projects of the earlier study.

The finding in the present study that differences in proximity to Negroes *within* a project seemed to be much more potent in leading to differential attitudes—policy orientation was an exception—than were differences in occupancy pattern suggests the desirability of comparing extreme proximity groups in the present projects with the respondents in the Deutsch and Collins integrated and segregated projects. In a sense, this procedure permits a direct replication of the proximity aspects of the Deutsch and Collins study, and is feasible because many of the questions asked were identical in both studies.

It would be possible to combine all the "nears" in the present study and compare them with the residents of the Deutsch and Collins integrated projects, and to compare all the "fars" with the residents of the Deutsch and Collins segregated projects. However, this would mean including among the "nears" many who did not live next door to Negroes, and including among the "fars" many who were not at any considerable distance. A better comparison is provided by considering, on the one hand, only those living *next door* to Negroes in the present projects (i.e., in Integrated I and Integrated II) and, on the other hand, only those living in *all-white areas* (whether in Building-Segregated I, Building-Segregated II, or Integrated II). There were 91 white respondents living next door to Negroes in the present projects (29 in Integrated I and 62 in Integrated II); these women may be thought of as corresponding to the white residents of the integrated projects in the Deutsch and Collins study. In the present projects there were 234 white respondents living in all-white areas relatively isolated from Negroes (95 in Building-Segregated I, 75 in Integrated II, and 64 in Building-Segregated II); in terms of proximity to Negroes, these women may be thought of as corresponding to the white residents of the area-segregated projects in the Deutsch and Collins study. It will be noted that *proximity* is being taken as the major variable here and that it cuts across lines of the official occupancy pattern in the case of the residents in all-white areas in Integrated II. These combinations of respondents also ignore the differences in situational factors and initial attitudes that were found between projects of like and unlike occupancy type in the present study. Insofar as these differences affect the extremes of the proximity groups, they would, of course, work against similarity of our findings with those of Deutsch and Collins.

Table 57 compares the extremes of the proximity groups of the present study with the Deutsch and Collins respondents in integrated and area-segregated projects in terms of level of contact with Negroes in the project. Although the Deutsch and Collins study did not use the com-

Table 57. A Comparison between the Respondents in the Deutsch and Collins Study and the Respondents in the Extremes of the Proximity Groups of the Present Study, on the Basis of the Level of Contact with Negroes in the Projects*

Percentage Sharing at Least One Kind of Neighborly Activity			
2 Integrated Projects of the Deutsch and Collins Study (192)	Integrated Projects of the Present Study † (91)	2 Segregated Projects of the Deutsch and Collins Study (201)	Segregated Areas of the Present Study ‡ (234)
54%	50%	3%	5%

* Data for the Deutsch and Collins study are taken from *Interracial Housing* (7). In this and the following tables, the percentages given for the Deutsch and Collins projects have been obtained by averaging the weighted percentages of the two integrated and of the two area-segregated projects.

† Next-door neighbors, Integrated I and II; respondents who resemble integrated project respondents of the Deutsch and Collins study.

‡ All-white courts and areas, Building-Segregated I and II and Integrated II; respondents who resemble segregated project respondents of the Deutsch and Collins study

plete scale of contact used in the present study, it did investigate the extent of *neighborly activities,* defined in exactly the same way as in the present study. As can be seen from the table, 54 per cent of the 192 respondents in the two Deutsch and Collins integrated projects reported participating in neighborly activities with Negroes; almost the same proportion—50 per cent—of the combined next-door neighbor groups in Integrated I and Integrated II reported such activities. At the other extreme, only 3 per cent of the 201 respondents in the two area-segregated projects of the Deutsch and Collins study reported such activities; similarly, only 5 per cent of the combined group living in all-white areas in Building-Segregated I, Building-Segregated II, and Integrated II reported participating in neighborly activities with Negroes. In extent of neighborly contact, then, the white women living next door to Negroes in the projects of the present study are almost identical with the white women in the integrated projects of the Deutsch and Collins study, and the women living in all-white areas in the projects of the present study (regardless of the official occupancy pattern) are almost identical with the women in the area-segregated projects of the Deutsch and Collins study.

Table 58 compares these groups with respect to perception of the social climate regarding interracial association in the project. Again, the responses of women living next door to Negroes in the present projects are similar to those of the women in the integrated projects of the Deutsch and Collins study, while those of women living in all-white areas are similar to those of women in the Deutsch and Collins

Table 58. A Comparison between the Respondents in the Deutsch and Collins Study and the Respondents in the Extremes of the Proximity Groups of the Present Study, on the Basis of Perception of the Social Climate within the Projects

Anticipated Reaction of White Friends in Project to Interracial Association	2 Integrated Projects of the Deutsch and Collins Study (192)	Integrated Projects of the Present Study * (91)	2 Segregated Projects of the Deutsch and Collins Study (201)	Segregated Areas of the Present Study † (234)
Unqualifiedly favorable	46%	37%	4%	15%
Mixed or neutral	26	22	21	9
Unfavorable	19	26	57	50
Don't know, not classifiable	9	15	18	26

* Next-door neighbors, Integrated I and II; respondents who resemble integrated project respondents of the Deutsch and Collins study.

† All-white courts and areas, Building-Segregated I and II and Integrated II; respondents who resemble segregated project respondents of the Deutsch and Collins study.

segregated projects. For example, in the integrated projects of the Deutsch and Collins study, 46 per cent of the respondents reported their friends as unqualifiedly favorable to interracial association, compared to 4 per cent in the area-segregated projects. In the present study, 37 per cent of the women living next door to Negroes and 15 per cent of those living in all-white areas reported their friends as favorable.

These similarities between the extremes of the proximity groups of the present study and the residents in the integrated and the segregated projects of the Deutsch and Collins study, with respect to neighborly activities and the perception of the informal social climate, would lead us to expect similarities in attitudes toward Negroes. Table 59 shows the proportions of respondents holding various degrees of "esteem" for the Negroes in the projects. It can be seen that the combined respondents living in all-white areas in the present projects were almost identical with the respondents in the Deutsch and Collins segregated projects: 41 per cent of both groups held Negroes in the project in high esteem; 37 per cent in the Deutsch and Collins segregated projects and 34 per cent in the all-white areas of the present projects held Negroes in low esteem.

Table 59. A Comparison between the Respondents in the Deutsch and Collins Study and the Respondents in the Extremes of the Proximity Groups of the Present Study, on the Basis of Degree of "Esteem" for Negroes in the Projects

Degree of Esteem	2 Integrated Projects of the Deutsch and Collins Study (192)	Integrated Projects of the Present Study * (91)	2 Segregated Projects of the Deutsch and Collins Study (201)	Segregated Areas of the Present Study † (234)
High	75%	56%	41%	41%
Mixed high and low.	13	22	22	19
Low	12	22	37	34
Not classifiable	...	...	...	6

*Next-door neighbors, Integrated I and II; respondents who resemble integrated project respondents of the Deutsch and Collins study.

†All-white courts and areas, Building-Segregated I and II and Integrated II; respondents who resemble segregated project respondents of the Deutsch and Collins study.

However, the correspondence between the combined next-door-neighbor groups of the present study and the respondents in the Deutsch and Collins integrated projects is less striking; 75 per cent of the combined respondents in the Deutsch and Collins integrated projects and 56 per cent of the next-door neighbors in the present projects expressed high esteem for Negroes. The reason why the average of the next-door-neighbor groups of the present study does not correspond more closely to the average of the integrated projects of the Deutsch and Collins study becomes clearer when the responses of the two next-door-neighbor groups of the present study are contrasted. While 76 per cent of the next-door neighbors in Integrated I hold Negroes in high esteem (almost identical with the respondents in the Deutsch and Collins integrated projects) not quite half of the next-door neighbors in Integrated II give the same response. The possible situational and initial-attitude reasons for the lower esteem on the part of residents of Integrated II have been discussed earlier.

The similarity between the extreme proximity groups of the present study and the integrated-project and segregated-project respondents of the Deutsch and Collins study emphasizes again the importance of proximity. It appears that one of the major ways in which the integrated occupancy pattern is conducive to more favorable attitudes is through greater proximity between Negro and white tenants. Where the proportion of Negroes is high, so that many white residents live next door to a Negro family, this factor is enhanced; where there are few Negroes, and thus few white families living directly next door to them, this factor is reduced. Material presented earlier, in connection with the discussion of differences between "nears" and "fars" *within* the same project, demonstrated that proximity directly influences the extent of interracial contact and the perception of social climate; these factors, in turn, influence various components of interracial attitude.

While it seems clear that the greater Negro-white proximity in an integrated project is one of the major factors contributing to the favorable influence of such a pattern, it would be an oversimplification to conclude that the differences between integrated and area-segregated projects found, for example, in the Deutsch and Collins study can be completely accounted for in terms of differences in Negro-white proximity. Our material clearly indicates the multiplicity of factors influencing the outcome—in particular, initial attitudes, situational factors (other than occupancy pattern) within the project, the effect of interpretation of the intentions of housing planners in adopting a given occupancy pattern, and the very considerable weight of general community atmosphere with respect to interracial association.

CHAPTER XI

A Brief Summary

In EACH of the projects studied in the course of this research, approximately 10 per cent of the families were Negro. Two of the projects were characterized by an integrated occupancy pattern and two by a building-segregated pattern. One of the integrated and one of the building-segregated projects were relatively new, located in small cities, had relatively small project populations, and were at a moderate income level. The other two projects were older, in large cities, had large project populations, and were at a low income level. None of the projects was within the metropolitan area of New York City, the nearest being 85 miles away.

Before our initiation of this study, the general conclusion regarding interracial contact and attitude change which seemed justified by earlier research and theory was as follows: The attitudes of the members of one racial group toward the members of another will tend to become more favorable if there is sufficient contact between the two groups, provided that (a) the contacts occur between individuals who do not differ markedly in their social status in the contact situation, and (b) the contacts do not occur under circumstances in which there is competition for limited goods or facilities.

This general conclusion is not only supported by the findings of the present study, but is amplified in several ways. We have, for instance, attempted to clarify the role that is played by living near the members of another ethnic group, to clarify the consequences of different occupancy patterns when the proportion of Negro families is small, to see how contact and social atmosphere interact in producing attitude change, and to determine whether the attitude changes are limited to certain kinds of attitude.

The major findings which give support to the general conclusion are outlined below.

1. *How do white residents, living relatively near to or far from Negro families in the same project, react to Negroes?*

147

Within each of the projects studied, *more* of those living near Negro families than of those living relatively far from them—

a) Have *some* kind of contact—i.e., at least exchange greetings with Negroes when passing on the street.

b) Have intimate contacts—i.e., visit back and forth, help one another out, etc.

c) Perceive the informal social climate as favorable to interracial association.

d) Have favorable attitudes with respect to their beliefs about the characteristics of the Negroes in the project, with respect to what their feelings are toward these Negroes, and with respect to their reactions to having white people live in the same community with Negroes.

e) Have favorable attitudes toward Negroes in general—i.e., not merely toward the Negroes living in the project.

2. Are the above differences due to the fact that those who are already more favorably disposed towards Negroes tend (or happen) to be the ones who move close to Negro families? Are the less favorably disposed more likely to move out of the project when located near Negro-occupied apartments? Or, may we infer instead that these differences result from living at greater or lesser distances from the Negro residents?

On the basis of several lines of evidence (known management rental practices, information from management about rejections of apartments offered, move-out rates, our own estimates of the respondents' initial attitudes based on objective data, and the respondents' own assessment of their initial attitudes), we may conclude that:

a) The above-mentioned differences cannot be accounted for in terms of differences in attitudes which already existed when the tenants moved in.

b) Nor can they be accounted for on the basis of differences in move-out rates.

It follows that either those living near Negroes have *changed* in the direction of having increased contact, more favorable attitudes, etc., or that *more* of them than of those living farther away have so changed. There is also direct testimony to such change from the tenants themselves, more of the "nears" than of the "fars" reporting a change in attitude. We may also conclude that these changes are associated with actually living in the projects.

3. Do these changes take place only in those residents who were more favorably disposed toward Negroes to begin with, or do they take place in both the more favorably and the less favorably disposed?

They take place in both groups regardless of initial disposition. Also, when we separate the initially less favorable from the initially more favorable, we find in each of these groups separately the same kinds of differences between the "nears" and the "fars" as have been reported above.

4. Do both contact and perceived social climate play a role in producing attitude change? If so, are their effects additive?

Each of these factors does play a role, and their effects are additive. When we consider separately the initially less favorable and the initially more favorable (whether they live relatively near to Negroes or farther away) we find that:

a) The more intimate the contact, the more favorable the attitudes.

b) The more favorable the perceived social climate surrounding interracial contact, the more favorable the attitudes.

c) When contact is intimate and the perceived social climate favorable, attitudes are most favorable; when contact is superficial and the perceived climate unfavorable, attitudes are least favorable; and when contact is intimate but the perceived social climate unfavorable, or when the contact is superficial and the perceived social climate favorable, the favorableness of the attitudes is intermediate.

5. Under the condition which prevailed in our projects—the small proportion of Negro families—is the integrated occupancy pattern more effective in changing attitudes than the building-segregated pattern?

Our findings on this point are inconsistent. They cannot be said to give a clearcut affirmative answer.

The relevant facts are as follows:

a) On most items, the differences between matched projects are small, sometimes tending to favor one and sometimes the other.

b) White residents in the building-segregated projects were less likely to express dissatisfaction with living in projects like the ones they were in.

c) More white residents in the integrated projects than in the building-segregated projects recommended completely segregated projects for future housing developments, but there were also more who recommended integrated occupancy patterns.

d) In all the projects, a majority of the respondents who were themselves dissatisfied with living in a mixed project recommended completely separate projects for future housing developments; but of those who were themselves satisfied with living in a mixed project, the majority in the integrated projects recommended the integrated pattern and the majority in the building-segregated projects recommended the building-segregated pattern for future housing developments.

6. Do these facts require that we reject the hypothesis that, under equal conditions, the integrated occupancy pattern has an advantage over the building-segregated pattern from the point of view of improving intergroup relations?

No, we do not need to reject the hypothesis. The reasons for the reversals of our expectations rested on the fact that some very relevant conditions proved to be not equal, and one which was expected to be unequal proved to be equal:

a) The "average" proximity of white to Negro families was not markedly different in the building-segregated than in the integrated projects. Thus, while there were some white residents in integrated projects who lived in the same building with Negro residents, there were at the same time a great many who lived farther away than did many white families in the building-segregated projects. This finding establishes the fact that given a small proportion of Negro families, differences in average proximity are not necessarily inherent in the two types of project.

b) Historical and situational factors tended to favor the buildingsegregated projects over their matched integrated projects from the point of view of good race relations.

c) The estimates of initial attitudes of the residents also indicated that the building-segregated projects started at an advantage.

d) To the extent that the preceding two findings truly reflect initially more unfavorable attitudes in the integrated projects, one possible implication of all three findings taken together is that the integrated occupancy pattern has to some extent overcome the initial difference favoring the building-segregated projects.

7. How do we interpret the effects of proximity, contact, and perceived social climate?

At this point we can only give what is probably an oversimplified version of the presumed process. Nearness of residence to Negroes increases the likelihood that a white resident will have at least casual contacts with Negroes; it does so directly through the increased probability of, so to speak, rubbing elbows, and it does so indirectly by increasing the probability of being drawn into contacts by white friends who are themselves more ready for such contacts. Nearness also increases the likelihood that the white resident will observe interracial association of Negroes and whites as a normal part of the social processes of the community and hence perceive a social climate favorable to such intermingling. If either of these likelihoods materializes, but especially when both do, the white resident's attitudes (i.e., beliefs, feelings, and policy orientations) adjust themselves to the new state of affairs so that another step can be taken toward somewhat less casual contact and/or appreciation of the normalcy of Negro-white association. This, in turn, may lead to a new readjustment of attitudes which, in its turn, may lead to a new forward step, and so on until some stable equilibrium of contact and favorable attitude is reached. The point at which the process stabilizes depends on the characteristics, interests, and values of the particular individuals involved, and possibly on whether the social atmosphere which sanctions contact begins to differentiate as particular levels of intimacy are reached.

In general, contact under the favorable conditions prevailing in the interracial public housing project may be assumed to provide concrete experiences which test the white resident's pre-existing stereotypes, and encourage the development of friendly relations and of the feelings appropriate to such relations. The perception by a white resident of the normalcy of association between Negro and white people on an equal status basis may be assumed, on the one hand, to require a readjustment of prior attitudes to the fact that Negroes are apparently the *kind of people* with whom it is proper for whites to associate, and, on the other hand, to eliminate the fear of censure, loss of status, or other undesirable consequences that association with Negroes might bring about in a prejudiced environment. Presumably, the same processes take place for the Negro residents.

Lastly, we may assume that when the white residents become less hostile to, suspicious or derogatory of Negroes, this change in attitude is perceived by their Negro neighbors and friendship between the races becomes more likely. Similarly, to the extent that Negro residents feel less suspicion and hostility toward whites, the Negroes also change in an objective sense, and the possibility of their becoming friends with their white neighbors increases. These processes, in turn, set up the conditions for further movement toward harmonious and cordial relations.

APPENDIX, BIBLIOGRAPHY
AND INDEX

Review of the Literature

AMONG the earliest studies of intergroup contact and attitude change were three which used experimental methods: those by Young (28), Williams (26), and F. T. Smith (22). In each case the interracial group was formed expressly for the purpose of improving attitudes toward Negroes (or of studying the effects of intergroup contact on attitudes); in each case participation was voluntary. In the study reported by Young, a group of white college students heard, as part of their course work, lectures by outstanding Negroes, visited a Negro hospital, etc.; the contacts occurred, apparently, once a week over the period of one semester. Williams brought 15 white girls and 23 Negro girls into contact in the course of YWCA club activity. Smith's study was based on a two-weekend (four-day) tour of Harlem by 46 white students at Columbia University. During these visits the students listened to lectures by prominent Negro leaders; met Negro doctors, scientists, writers; were entertained in an upper-class Negro home. The Negro and white girls in the Williams study may be considered similar not only in general socioeconomic status but in their roles in the club activity. In the Young and Smith studies, the Negroes presumably were of somewhat higher status than the white students, since they not only were individuals of outstanding accomplishments but also occupied something of a teaching position in relation to the students. The relative status of the groups having contact is stressed at this point because of the conviction, to be developed shortly, that the status relations help to determine the outcomes of the contacts.

In all three studies, before-and-after measures of attitudes were used. Young reported very little improvement in attitude toward Negroes on the part of his white students. Since the study is, unfortunately, only sketchily reported, it is difficult to determine what measuring instruments were used and just how much change was observed. Williams, on the other hand, found a significant improvement in the attitudes of the white girls participating in the interracial club. Smith used, in addition to before-and-after measurement, a control group of matched students who had also expressed interest in participating in the Harlem tour. Employing a variety of attitude scales, he found substantial improvement on the part of those who had been on the Harlem trips and no improvement on the part of the control students; moreover, the improvement in attitude of those who had participated in the trips was largely maintained ten months later.

In addition to these few experimental investigations, there have been a number of studies in which respondents' present attitudes were compared with their own reports of prior contact with minority group members. Allport and Kramer (3), for example, questioned white college students about their prior experience with Negroes and about their present attitudes toward Negroes. They found that while *any* contact with Negroes was more likely to be related to favorable attitudes than was no contact at all, certain types of contact more than others were related to favorable attitudes. The contacts most highly related to favorable attitude were those which occurred in school, at work, in recreation, as neighbors, and as friends. Allport and Kramer consider the essential characteristic of these contacts to be that of equal status on the part of the Negro and white participants.

Mackenzie (16) had college students and government employees fill out a questionnaire which measured present attitude and asked about prior contact with Negroes. She found that favorable attitudes toward Negroes were associated with contacts with Negroes who had "high status," i.e., were college students or professional people, such as doctors, lawyers, or teachers, whereas contact with Negroes of nonprofessional status tended to be associated with less favorable attitudes. Since the subjects answering the questionnaire had themselves a relatively high economic and educational status, this could be interpreted as supporting the view that equal-status contacts tend to be associated with more favorable attitudes.

Watson (25), in a study devoted to determining some conditions conducive to attitude change, conducted intensive interviews with 45 non-Jewish subjects who reported having undergone changes—either favorable or unfavorable—in attitudes toward Jews or Negroes. While the number of cases is small, her findings also support the general hypothesis that equal-status contact is associated with favorable attitudes. Of 23 respondents who had had contact with Negroes or Jews of "at least equal status" to that of the respondent, 21 were classified as having altered their attitudes in a more favorable direction. Of 14 respondents who had had contact with Negroes or Jews of lower status than themselves, 10 had changed in attitude in an unfavorable direction.

Merton, West, and Jahoda (17), in a study focused primarily on attitudes as related to the experience of living in a biracial public housing project, also considered the question of prior contact with Negroes. Respondents who reported *both* work and residential experience with Negroes before moving into the project were more likely to approve of biracial living than were respondents who had had only one type of contact (either work *or* residential); those who reported *one* of these types of contact were, in turn, more likely to approve of biracial living than those who had had neither job nor prior neighborhood experiences with Negroes. The status aspects of these experiences is not specified; however, it may be inferred that for many of the white respondents contacts were with Negroes of approximately equal economic status.

Saenger and Flowerman (20), in a study of the relation between stereotypes and other dimensions of attitude, considered the relation between contact and various dimensions of prejudice. They found that, while persons who had had "much" contact with Jews showed greater willingness to associate with them than those who had had "no" contact, this was not true of persons with "moderate" amounts of contact.

The evidence from these non-experimental studies and others that are similar seems to establish quite conclusively a relationship between contact, particularly of an equal-status character, and favorable attitudes. However, this finding is difficult to interpret, since these studies include little or no evidence as to the direction of the causal sequence. It may be that the contacts led to attitude change. On the other hand, the possibility must be considered that the contacts were undertaken (or at least not avoided) because the individuals who experienced them were originally favorably disposed to the minority in question. The authors cited are aware of this problem. The difficulty can only be overcome when further analysis is possible which may reveal the direction of the causal sequence.

It has been possible to conduct a number of ex post facto studies of the effects of contact in "real life" situations where the nature of the contact is known, and where initial attitudes can at least be estimated from other known characteristics of the subjects or from the logic of the situation. In a World War II study reported in *The American Soldier* (24), white combat infantrymen in units of varying organizational distance (and so, physical distance) from Negro platoons were questioned about their reaction to the idea of having Negro and white soldiers serve in the same units. It was found that the soldiers most favorable to Negro-white units were those in companies which already had a volunteer Negro platoon. Next most favorable were soldiers in all-white companies in regiments which had one or more Negro-white companies. Least favorable were soldiers in all-white companies in all-white regiments. There is no direct information in the original report of this study about the initial attitudes of the white soldiers. However, as Kendall and Lazarsfeld (12) point out in a reexamination of the findings of this study, the Negro platoons had been assigned to companies on the basis of military need, without consulting the white soldiers about their willingness to serve with Negroes. Thus it seems unlikely that white soldiers in units physically closer to Negro platoons were different in initial attitudes from those in units farther away.

Two studies in public housing projects having both Negro and white residents report findings similar to those of the study presented in *The American Soldier*. Merton, West, and Jahoda (17) studied a low-rental, building-segregated housing project in which the over-all Negro-white ratio was about 50 to 50. The project was divided, however, into three terraces, in which the proportions of Negroes were 63 per cent, 44 per cent, and 0 per cent respectively. In the first two terraces, the Negro-occupied buildings were interspersed among the white-occupied buildings. These investigators found that both the number of white respondents reporting friendships with Negroes and the number expressing approval of biracial living were greatest in the terrace having the highest proportion of Negroes, next greatest in the terrace where 44 per cent of the tenants were Negroes, and smallest in the all-white terrace. Although there was no conclusive evidence as to the initial attitudes of the white tenants in the three terraces, there seemed no reason to suppose that they had differed significantly, since the assignments to dwelling units in the various terraces were not based on tenants' choices. In the terrace with the highest proportion of Negroes there were, of course, the greatest proportion of white tenants living in close proximity to a Negro-occupied building. Here, it may be inferred, the most frequent occasions arose for contact between members of the two races. The conclusion seems justified, therefore, that greater proximity and more frequent contact led to the development both of more friendships between white and Negro tenants and of more favorable attitudes on the part of the white tenants toward biracial living.

In the other study of public housing projects, Deutsch and Collins (7) investigated in great detail the relation between occupancy pattern (including Negro-white proximity), the incidence of contact between the races, and attitudes. Four low-rental public housing projects were studied, in each of which Negroes constituted not less than 40 per cent of the total project population. Two of the projects were of integrated occupancy pattern, in which a majority of white tenants lived next door to Negro families in the same apartment buildings. Two were area-segregated, the Negro and white sections being separated from each other in one case by a busy street, in the other by a large play area for children. The authors found marked differences between the two types of projects in a number of respects. The white residents in the integrated projects reported more frequently that white tenants "would be likely to get to know" colored people there and that they themselves engaged in neighborly contacts with Negro tenants, such as exchanging services and friendly visiting. Moreover, the white residents in the integrated projects were more likely than those in the area-segregated projects to hold Negroes in the project in high "esteem," were less likely to hold unfavorable stereotypes of Negroes, and were less likely to want to avoid contact with the Negroes in the project. They were more likely to accept the biracial character of the project and to recommend an integrated occupancy pattern for future projects. A far greater proportion in the integrated projects reported that they had undergone favorable attitude change as a consequence of living in the project. Finally, there was evidence of some generalization of the experience; the white residents in the integrated projects were more likely than those in the area-segregated projects to be favorable in their appraisal of Negroes in general as well as of the specific Negroes living in the project.

Deutsch and Collins also attempted to estimate the degree of similarity of initial attitudes of the white tenants in the different types of projects by comparing them on factors known to be correlated with initial attitude, such as religion, educational level, political liberalism or conservatism, and prior knowledge of the biracial character of the project. They concluded that while the tenants in the integrated projects might initially have been somewhat more favorably disposed toward Negroes than those in the area-segregated projects, the difference in predisposition was not sufficient to account for the marked differences existing in behavior and attitude at the time of the study. It appeared that the difference in occupancy pattern was the primary factor leading to differences both in amount of contact and in favorableness of attitude.

Studies of residential proximity in other settings have had somewhat different findings. Kramer (14) conducted a study of white residents of five small contiguous residential areas in Chicago. In one area ("Zone 1"), Negro and white dwelling units were found in the same block. The Negroes had moved into this block relatively recently. The remaining four areas contained no Negro residents, and varied in distance from the Negro-white zone. Zone 2 (a strip three blocks wide) lay directly south of Zone 1; Zone 3 (also three blocks wide) was directly south of Zone 2, etc. Kramer interpreted these differences in proximity as representing differences in amount of *contact* between Negroes and whites, without obtaining direct evidence concerning the nature of Negro-white face-to-face contacts which occurred. It seems to the present authors that it would be more cautious to treat his areas as differing systematically in *proximity* to the Negro-white zone, rather than in the amount of biracial contact. Kramer found that the relationships between proximity and attitude differed, depending on the attitude dimension considered. Thus, on a scale of prejudice constructed for the study he found the least prejudice in Zones 1 and 5—the zones where white residents lived *nearest to* and *farthest from* Negroes— and the most prejudice in the zones of intermediate proximity. A possible interpretation seems to be that those in the zone farthest from Negroes represented an "average" degree of prejudice—that is, the attitude of the typical Chicago resident not faced with the prospect of having Negro neighbors. According to this interpretation residents of the three intermediate zones may be thought of as having undergone an increase in prejudice as a consequence of feeling "threatened" by the impending closeness of Negroes. The actual experience of living in the same block as neighbors evidently reduced the anticipatory fears, and brought the attitudes of the white residents of Zone 1 back to— but not below—the "average" degree of prejudice shown in Zone 5.

With regard to salience of the racial issue, however, Kramer found a different pattern. There was a consistent linear relationship between proximity to Negroes and the likelihood of prejudiced statements being made spontaneously, those living close to Negroes being the *most* inclined to voice such statements. On the other hand, there was a linear relationship in the reverse direction between proximity and the desire to resist Negro movement into the neighborhood, whites living farthest away being most inclined to resist such movement. Data on education, age, religious background, and home ownership showed no significant differences between the zones which would suggest differences in attitudinal predispositions.

Winder (27), in a similarly designed study of neighborhoods in Chicago which were in varying degrees of proximity to an area Negroes had recently moved into, found differentiating factors of another sort. He too reported, for the sample as a whole, least prejudice on the part of those *closest to* and *farthest from* Negroes. Breaking down his sample in terms of socioeconomic groupings, however, he found that it was only in the middle-income group that residents in the area closest to Negroes showed less prejudice than those in the intermediate zones. The low-income whites in the area closest to Negroes were even more hostile than those in the intermediate zones. Winder concluded, on the basis of interview responses, that the hostility of the low-income white residents was based on competition for dwelling units in the midst of a severe housing shortage. These white residents felt—evidently on the basis of objective evidence—that owners of multiple dwellings were eager to force them out because higher rents could be demanded from Negroes (who, of course, suffer even more severely from housing shortage).

The Winder and the Kramer studies, together with several surveys using less detailed measurement of resistance to Negro entry into previously white neighborhoods, such as Long's *People vs. Property* (15), point to a number of factors which must be taken into account in any discussion of the effects of proximity on intergroup attitudes. The studies are interesting not only for their demonstration that different dimensions of attitude, and different groups of respondents, may be differently affected. Even more important is the fact that they are concerned with situations of racial movement under conditions where the coming of Negroes is seen by the earlier residents as a threat to their status, and where there may even be actual competition for sorely needed living quarters. Such situations, of course, are quite different from those investigated by Merton, West, and Jahoda (17), by Deutsch and Collins (7), and in the study reported in *The American Soldier* (24). These last studies, as well as the present study, deal with relatively stable and self-contained situations, in which Negroes and whites have approximately equal status, where there are few factors in the objective situation making for competition between members of the two groups and numerous factors making for cooperation, and where there is less reason for one group to view the other's presence as a threat.

Bibliography

1. Ackerman, N. W., and Marie Jahoda. *Anti-Semitism and Emotional Disorder.* New York: Harper, 1950.
2. Adorno, T. W., Else Frenkel-Brunswik, D. J. Levinson, and R. N. Sanford. *The Authoritarian Personality.* New York: Harper, 1950.
3. Allport, G. W., and B. M. Kramer. "Some Roots of Prejudice," *J. Psychol.,* 1946, 22:9–39.
4. Chein, I. "What Are the Psychological Effects of Segregation under Conditions of Equal Facilities?" *Int. J. Opin. Att. Res.,* 1949, 3:229–34.
5. ———. "Notes on a Framework for the Measurement of Discrimination and Prejudice," in Marie Jahoda, M. Deutsch, and S. W. Cook, *Research Methods in Social Relations,* I, 382–90. New York: Dryden, 1951.
6. Dean, J. P. Unpublished study of intergroup relations, 1951 (part of the Cornell University Community Studies).
7. Deutsch, M., and Mary E. Collins. *Interracial Housing: A Psychological Evaluation of a Social Experiment.* Minneapolis: University of Minnesota Press, 1951.
8. Festinger, L., and H. H. Kelly. *Changing Attitudes through Social Contact.* Ann Arbor, Mich.: Research Center for Group Dynamics, University of Michigan, 1951.
9. Festinger, L., S. Schachter, and K. Back. *Social Pressures in Informal Groups.* New York: Harper, 1950.
10. Ford, R. N. "A Rapid Scoring Procedure for Scaling Attitude Questions," *Publ. Opin. Quar.,* 1950, 14:507–32.
11. Horowitz, E. L. "The Development of Attitude toward the Negro," *Arch. Psychol.* (New York), 1936, No. 194.
12. Kendall, Patricia L., and P. F. Lazarsfeld. "Problems of Survey Analysis," in R. K. Merton and P. F. Lazarsfeld, eds., *Continuities in Social Research.* New York: Free Press, 1950.
13. Kennedy, R. "Premarital Residential Propinquity," *Amer. J. Sociol.,* 1943, 48:580–84.
14. Kramer, B. M. "Residential Contact as a Determinant of Attitudes toward Negroes." Unpublished Ph.D. dissertation, Harvard University, 1951.
15. Long, H. H., and C. S. Johnson. *People vs. Property,* Nashville, Tenn.: Fisk University Press, 1947.
16. Mackenzie, Barbara K. "The Importance of Contact in Determining Attitudes toward Negroes," *J. Abn. Soc. Psychol.,* 1948, 43:417–41.
17. Merton, R. K., Patricia S. West, and Marie Jahoda. *Social Facts and Social Fictions: The Dynamics of Race Relations in Hilltown.* Hectographed, New York: Columbia University Bureau of Applied Social Research, June 1949. (Part of a larger work to be published under the title *Patterns of Social Life: Explorations in the Social Psychology and Sociology of Housing.*)
18. Mussen, P. H. "Some Personality and Social Factors Related to Change in Children's Attitudes toward Negroes," *J. Abn. Soc. Psychol.,* 1950, 45:423–41.

19. Newcomb, T. M. *Personality and Social Change.* New York: Dryden, 1943.

20. Saenger, G., and S. H. Flowerman. "Stereotypes and Prejudiced Attitudes," *Hum. Relat.,* in press.

21. Selltiz, Claire, S. W. Cook, and R. Hogrefe. "The Experience Survey: A Step in Program Design for Field Research in Unexplored Problems." Unpublished paper.

22. Smith, Fred Tredwell. *An Experiment in Modifying Attitudes toward the Negro* ("Contributions to Education," No. 887). New York: Columbia University Teachers College, 1943.

23. Smith, M. B. "The Personal Setting of Public Opinions: A Study of Attitudes toward Russia," *Publ. Opin. Quar.,* 1947, 11:507–23.

24. Stouffer, S. A., E. A. Suchman, L. C. DeVinney, Shirley A. Star, and R. M. Williams, Jr. *The American Soldier: Adjustment during Army Life* (Vol. I of *Studies in Social Psychology in World War II*). Princeton: Princeton University Press, 1950.

25. Watson, Jeanne. "Some Social and Psychological Situations Related to Change in Attitude," *Hum. Relat.,* 1950, 3:15–56.

26. Williams, D. H. "The Effects of an Interracial Project upon the Attitudes of Negro and White Girls within the Young Women's Christian Association." Unpublished M.A. thesis, Columbia University, 1934.

27. Winder, A. E. "White Attitudes toward Negro-White Interaction in an Area of Changing Racial Composition," *Amer. Psychol.,* 1952, 7:330–31 (abstract).

28. Young, D. *American Minority Peoples.* New York: Harper, 1932.

Index

Ackerman, N. W., 9n
Acquaintance, process of growing, and attitude change, 109–10. *See also* Interracial contact.
Adorno, T. W., 9n, 62n, 76
Allport, G. W., 156
Average proximity of white to Negro tenants, 114, 130–31

Back, K., 7
Beliefs about minority groups, 4, 5, 48, 49
Beliefs in equality of Negroes and whites in the project: and proximity, 49, 50–51; and contact, 99, 100; and perceived social climate, 102, 103; and interrelation between contact and social climate, 106, 107; and occupancy pattern, 120–21, 125
Building arrangement in projects, 17, 18, 19, 20: as related to effects of occupancy pattern, 135, 137

California Ethnocentrism Scale: and proximity, 62–64; and interrelation of proximity and initial attitude, 86, 87, 88, 90; and contact, 99, 100; and social climate, 102, 103; and interrelation of contact and social climate, 106, 107; and occupancy pattern, 121–22, 136
Chein, I., 4n
Children: as topics of interracial conversation, 36, 37; amount of interracial contact, 37–38; values seen by parents in biracial living, 57, 123; respondents' attitudes toward biracial play, 57, 123
Chinese. *See* Racial attitudes.
Coding: reliability of, 25; safeguard against bias of, 25
Collins, Mary E. *See* Deutsch and Collins study.
Community atmospheres, 133, 134, 137–38

Comparability of respondents. *See* Initial comparability.
Contact. *See* Interracial contact.
Cook, S. W., 12

Dean, J. P., 9n
Deutsch and Collins study, 4n, 5n, 8, 9, 10, 11, 12, 14–17, 22, 24, 26, 113–15, 127n, 131, 133n, 140, 141, 142–46, 158–59, 161
Deutsch, M. *See* Deutsch and Collins study.

Education, 75–76, 81, 133
Equal status contact. *See* Interracial contact.
Esteem for Negroes in the project: affected by experiences, 49; and proximity, 51–53; and interrelation of proximity and initial attitude, 86, 87, 89, 90; and contact, 97–98, 99, 100; and social climate, 102, 103; and interrelation of contact and social climate, 106, 107; and occupancy pattern, 120, 121, 135, 136, 140; present findings compared with Deutsch and Collins findings, 145–46
Ethnocentrism Scale. *See* California Ethnocentrism Scale.
Evaluation of biracial experiences as pleasant or unpleasant: and proximity, 38–40; and occupancy pattern, 116

Feelings about living in biracial projects: and proximity, 53–58; and interrelation of proximity and initial attitude, 86, 87, 90; and contact, 99, 100; and social climate, 102, 103; and interrelation of contact and social climate, 106, 107; and occupancy pattern, 122–23, 135, 137, 140; relation to policy orientation, 124–27

164